# Of Berries and Scones

## On Any Given Day

# Gina Tan

Christian Musings For The Living

PARTRIDGE

A Penguin Random House Company

**To order additional copies of this book, contact**
Toll Free 800 101 2657 (Singapore)
Toll Free 1 800 81 7340 (Malaysia)
orders.singapore@partridgepublishing.com

www.partridgepublishing.com/singapore

# Contents

*This very readable book of musings on the daily life is just what it is. Written by a daughter, mother, wife and most importantly as a follower of Jesus Christ brings a perspective that is both endearing and true. The beauty of the book is how the Word of God is central as Gina courageously addresses issues on wrong thinking and behavior. You will find issues addressed that many want to talk about but not felt safe to do so. Reflecting on these writings can only help us walk with God rightly as Gina points us to God again and again and expresses so confidently her trust and hope in the living God.*

*Alan & Connie Ch'ng*
*International Vice President*
*The Navigators*

*Quirky stories to make you smile, pointed questions to help examine your life, and sharing of much joy in living out a full life. Good scone recipes too, but we all know the secret lies in the making of scones, so I'll just have to invite myself over.*

*Poh Lerk Shih*
*Christian Feminist, Eschet Chayil*

For

*Rebekah*
*Hannah*
*Joshua*

my inspiration
my pride
my joy

# Acknowledgements

I am thankful for my family, the earthly strength of my life's zeal; my husband Michael for his prayer covering and my children Rebekah, Hannah and Joshua for their pushing me out to the field and cheering me on on numerous occasions.

I can always remember my student days when my father said that English and Math were two very important subjects to pay attention to. I grew up learning to love reading and writing essays and that never stopped. My mother has always been the best mother anyone could ask for; a beauty on the outside and even more on the inside who taught me that a mother is a person who is always there for her family. I am thankful I was born to my parents.

I thank my friends who encouraged me to bring my writings to the printers. I especially thank Mona Loh who had badger eyes needing wolf berry supplements when her proof-reading job was done. And what is a book without a captivating cover picture! What a work well done, my friend and book cover illustrator Belle Chai.

Where would I be and what could I have done without my God—the Father, the Son and the Holy Spirit—who is my strength, my friend . . . . my ALL!

# Introduction

When I started saving my writings eights years ago, I never thought or dreamt that they would, one day, be compiled and come out from the printer's as a book. I am no big writer like some whose books I have read, but what has been impressed upon me, I share.

*OF BERRIES AND SCONES: On Any Given Day* is like how I share it to the women, young couples, children (to start with, my own) and anyone who I minister to, as illustration, discussion or lesson objective. These writings are my own reflections on happenings I see around me. It is my prayer that this book will inspire, teach, affirm, and do whatever good it can for your life in God.

As I bring you into my life and all that surround me as you read a chapter a day, I wish you His greatest gift, and that is knowing Jesus Christ as your personal Lord and Savior. God bless you!

p/s An ideal way to have a personal read or sharing it with your friends or small group is to do it while enjoying your favorite berries with a couple of scones.

Mixed dried fruits scones
Butter
Fresh strawberries
Green tea

# 1

# Letting Go Of Your Sheets

The sound of rain, the feel of slight cool breeze, and a comfortable bed can make even a morning person wish there were five more hours before wake time. That was exactly the scene I was caught in yesterday morning. The culprits: the rain and the cool breeze. The victim: me. Have you been in a similar situation—five more minutes, and when the five minutes are up, there is still time . . . . so five more minutes—where you feel like the sheets are slowly being pulled and dragged from the tight grip of your clenched fists. Your eyes are still closed; you are savouring closed eyes till the final second when you feel the last bits of the sheets' corners finally escape your hold. Ok, maybe this is just a little more dramatically imagined but you know what I mean.

I would have given almost anything for a little more sleep yesterday morning because the flesh was ready to give in to the lure of the cool weather but there was a firm nudge in my inner man that reminded me of the needs of my family, the chores, and my appointments for which I need to prepare.

An uncomplicated situation that seems agonizing as a result of one stepping out of comfort zone for the sake of others. But not all is seen from a bad perspective. I have received various lessons from people who dared to leave their comfort zone in the name of faith, justice, redemption, salvation, and more. When God said to Abram to go out of his country (Genesis 12-15) from his father's house, to some kind of forsaken land, Abram could have ignored God's call and stayed on in his father's house to keep enjoying his comfortable surroundings and all that he owned. But Abram decided to heed that call and departed as the LORD has spoken to him. He didn't know what to expect; how the land looked like or what his neighborhood would be like. He walked on with his family and possessions until God told him he had reached that land. He did this in the name of faith. Because of his faith, and doubtlessly obedience too, he was in the end blessed thousands of times more than where he was before. Through the blessings, up to today, countless are affirmed of the one true and living God's love.

Moses could have stayed on with his father-in-law Jethro. After all, with dad as priest, Moses could have taken delight in the position of son-in-law of the priest of Midian. Although

Moses expressed great uncertainty about whether he would be accepted by the Israelites as their God-intended leader, he did the unimaginable, facing his fears head on. Then God renewed His promise to the Israelites (Exodus 3-6).

Jonah, on the other hand, suited for an adventure, messed with the authority of the Almighty God. When God called him to carry out un unpopular task, the real shape of his heart was revealed. He fled. In foolishness, he thought he could hide from God. After stormy and fishy situations fraught with perils, Jonah decided he had had enough. He started preaching God's message of repentance and Nineveh repented.

Today, you could have received instructions you know so well are from God and probably struggling with the need to leave your comfort zone. It could be your pride you need to let go to say sorry for a relationship to be renewed. It could be that you have to leave your home, church, or country to undertake a purposeful assignment. It could also mean letting go of conveniences so that your loved ones can have a better life. It is perhaps time to let go of your sheets.

*Don't stay too long in a spiritually torpid state. Hibernation is more suited for the polar bear.*

# 2

# In Christian Comradeship

Wednesday mid afternoon saw me coming home feeling tired from a very hot and humid day . . . . but it was worth it. The 8 hours of strictly-ladies-only time with four other ladies went by too fast. Free from everything and everyone else, we let out hair down, ready to hit the road by 7.30am with a good appetite for a fun-filled day. We share a background of career woman-turned-housewife status which makes it easier for us to bond whenever we meet. The day was filled with laughter, mouthwatering food and some gutsy mid-age feat. As we sat down for lunch, I realised that above all the enjoyment we were having together, sharing our lives, pouring out our hearts and encouraging each other in the Lord made up the crowning moment of being together like this.

How many times situations had turned awry because one did not receive encouragement and support from fellow believers?

How many times decisions could have been better if only a couple of Christian buddies were there with sound advice? If we think that we can live this life shutting others out and staying away from Christian fellowships, we are only doing injustice to ourselves and to others. It can be upsetting to see believers falter in their hope in God. It saddens me when a sister or a brother makes decisions that loosen their hold in Him who has promised us the Light that will never diminish. But I don't blame this sister or brother entirely because sometimes one can be so caught in an overwhelming situation that focus is blurred. A couple of small problems when fed with unhealthy thoughts and emotions will likely give birth to illogical thinking.

When we decline Paul's advice in Hebrews 10:23-25, "Let us hold fast the confession of our hope without wavering, for He who promised is faithful, and let us consider one another in order to stir up love and good works, not forsaking the assembling of ourselves together, as in the manner of some, but exhorting one another, and so much the more as you see the Day approaching.", we are also neglecting the fact that we, believers, are all the Church, which is the Body of Christ. "And the eye cannot say to the hand, 'I have no need of you'; nor again the head to the feet, 'I have no need of you.'" (1 Corinthians 12:21). In Hebrews, the Jews who had earlier confessed Jesus as their Lord and Savior were starting to falter in their faith. The persecution they had to endure was probably too great a pressure for them to handle. The author reassure them of God's faithfulness and pointed out to them the cruciality of being part of the Christian assembly for a continuous Christian walk.

To need is part of being human. When needs are not being met in crucial areas, it is just a matter of time before the pressure gets too much to handle. We need God in all areas of our lives here on earth and He provides ways for His children to escape the ugly insults of the world. He gives us the assurance and wisdom of His Word, the peace, guidance and protection from His Holy Spirit, and He connects us with each other in Christian fellowship. If you are tottering down the path in life where a situation has turned sour, or if you are unsure on the edge of overwhelmingness, come to Him who is faithful and come for Christian fellowship.

As if the 8 hours were not enough, we met up again the following day; this time with our respective husbands and children for a sumptuous heritage lunch, more photos, and needless to say, a great time of fellowship! Oh, how I love the wonderful joy of Christian fellowship . . . . don't you?

*Give a call to a friend (or friends) and plan a get-together. If you haven't done anything of this sort for a long time, you will be surprised at how an amazing good change this will do to you.*

# 3

# Big N, Small N

Many centuries ago, a Chaldean Babylonian king named Nebuchadnezzar (let's call him 'Big N') was at the peak of his governing success when he gave instructions to his eunuch chief to give daily provisions of the king's delicacies to chosen wise, knowledgable and talented young men, preparing them to serve him (Daniel 1:5). In the second year of his reign, Big N had dreams that left him troubled. In his desperation to know what the dreams meant, he gave an unreasonable request, that any wise man who could not interpret his dream would be put to death (Daniel 2:8,9,12).

Then Big N decided to have a huge image made of gold. During the dedication of the image, everyone present was ordered to fall down and worship it. Whoever failed to do so would be immediately thrown into a burning furnace, which was a common practice of punishment in old Babylon (Daniel 3:6).

It is not a surprise if force, intimidation, destroying and killing are part of any ungodly style of government. Any wrongdoing, sometimes to the height of doing it unashamedly, bears no proof of blameworthiness anymore. If truth be told, there is no stability of principle in the ungodly. Government is a system by which a nation, state, or community is led. It is a manner of controlling or regulating an aggregate of people. We need a government to move toward betterment, not deterioration; to be protected, not to be instilled with twisted fear. The control part of the government is to be understood as for the benefit of the people.

Amidst the governing craze of Big N, there were these young men from Judah—Daniel, Shadrach, Meshach and Abed-nego who had an unhesitating decision to be indifferent toward any ruling from Big N which deemed to be wrongful according to their God's standard. "Daniel purposed in his heart not to defile himself with the king's delicacies" (Daniel 1:8), and the result proved that Big N's instruction was futile. Then God used Daniel to make Himself known and be reminded among the people (Daniel 2:36-45). He worked through Daniel to interpret Big N's dream which earned Daniel a big promotion to ruler of the whole province of Babylon and chief administrator to her wise men. Although they were considered as Big N's guys by now, they still stood their grounds as believers and followers of their God. They refused to bow down to Big N's gold image (Daniel 3:12,18).

A decree is a decree—Daniel and his friends were thrown into the burning furnace, with the heat turned up seven times more than usual. They came through the whole fiery perils unscathed! These four young men foiled Big N's word, stood their grounds, and opened the people's eyes that in the end, only God will have the final say. There is no ruler or government that is too big for His mighty arm. "These will make war with the Lamb, and the Lamb will overcome them, for He is Lord of lords, and King of kings, and those who are with Him are called, chosen, and faithful" (Revelation 17:14). World dominance will in the end have to acknowledge this. "And He has on His robe and on His thigh a name written: KING OF KINGS AND LORD OF LORDS" (Revelation 19:16).

Big N, who had before robbed God of His honor, eyes opened, realised that ". . . . the Most High rules in the kingdom of men, and gives it to whomever He chooses'" (Daniel 4:25), and that "'those who walk in pride He is able to put down'" (verse 37).

One day nations will declare that, "'blessed be the God of Shadrach, Meshach and Abed-nego, Who sent His angel and delivered His servants who trusted in Him, and they have frustrated the king's word, and yielded their bodies, that they should not serve nor worship any God except their own God! Therefore I make a decree that any people, nation, or language which speaks anything amiss against the God of

Shadrach, Meshach, and Abed-nego shall be cut in pieces, and their houses shall be made an ash heap; because there is no other God who can deliver like this."' (Daniel 3:28,29).

*"Lord, help us to live this life to be counted as the Daniel, Shardrach, Meshach and Abed-nego of today. Amen."*

# 4

# At Your Service

With a few areas to look into, I'm still in contemplating mode on whether I should give the children church ministry in a local church a go. I'm prepared to spend some time to pray and think about it because the ministry's leader approached me about joining her team and she did it in a sensible Christian way. She shared about the few reasons which prompted her to ask me to consider serving in the ministry. She also briefly told me about the vision and mission of the ministry.

I had a different experience some time ago which still is appalling to me when i think about it. My family and I were checking out a church which placed an emphasis on its choir. One day, after being there for some months, a leader suggested that I should join the choir. I answered that I would want some time to know the church better before I got too involved. She said, "What if you die tomorrow? Then you'd have no chance to sing in the choir." I grimaced a bit and asked her the logic for that way of talking. She was quick to reply that, as a Christian I should not have been superstitious when she said I were to die the next day. Of course, I was not being superstitious but rather taken aback by such a befuddling manner of encouraging someone to serve in Church. I hope singing in a church choir is indeed considered serving God!

If the decision to serve is born of obsession in power, being forced or made to feel guilty, or simply to draw attention to one's ability, then our intentions are due for a review. When there is a calling to serve in a certain ministry in Church, God will put His peace in our heart to do it. I don't think God expects us to just drop our nets and follow in every situation. Sometimes we may need to pray about it and see if that is the way we should go on. Sometimes we may want to try out the work or ministry for a while to see if that is the area of service for us. Some people need to be encouraged to go into a certain work in Church, and this should be done in *agape*. Many times through the years, I was asked to start or facilitate or help in something. I did not accept all requests or invites, and I did not feel guilty to those I said no to. Those I accepted, I felt the joy in doing it. Although some of the work took my precious time away from my personal agenda, God allowed me to see a diversion of my time's preciousness— lives were touched. Praise God!

In certain instances, the Spirit may put a burden in our heart to make the first step in approaching a person or ministry and say we want to serve. As God has given each one of us a gift (1 Peter 4:10-11), our heart may be stirred up to want to use that gift to also start a ministry. We can use our gifts to serve other people too. A good example is Dorcas (Acts 9:36-42) who is known as the lady full of good works. Matthew 25:40—"And the King will answer and say to them, 'Assuredly, I say to you, inasmuch as you did it to one of the least of these, My brethren, you did it to Me.'" What a beautiful God. First, He places importance to humankind, even to the least to all statuses. Then He makes sure that whatever His children serve in or give to others is taken into record. These deeds are considered done to God Himself, and are accepted as something pleasing to Him.

An excerpt from Os Hillman's 'Called To Ministry': We have incorrectly elevated the role of the Christian worker that serves within the church or a traditional ministry role to be more holy and committed than the person who is serving in the secular environment. Yet the call to the secular workplace is as important as any other calling. God has to have His people in every sphere of life to meet the needs of His creation. Also, many would never come to know Him because they would be separated from society.

About Christian service, we know that we are to serve; we encourage each other to serve; we thankfully accept service from others. Wherever God has put us, do all these with Christian integrity.

Because of One who served sacrificially, I have been redeemed. Matthew 20:28—". . . . just as the Son of Man did not come to be served, but to serve, and to give His life a ransom for many." Thank You, Jesus!

*A non-secret when serving: serve God, not man.*

# 5
# Spiritual F1

At the risk of sounding like a road menace, I confess that as a young car driver decades ago, I enjoyed leaving other back cars way behind. It was not on a F1 circuit but a normal road traffic lights junction. My careful calculation got me a *nyahahaha* satisfaction. If I spotted a distracted driver in the car at the back of mine at a red light—putting on makeup, tidying passenger seat or whatever that might seem like the driver taking his eyes and mind off the lights—i would not start driving yet when our light turned green . . . . until the car in front had driven off a good many meters away . . . . then i drove off. the driver in the back car would usually still be busy with whatever he was doing, and at the count of 1 2 3 there would start an orchestra of honks.

I have seen one, I have seen a few, and it irks me that in Christian ministries there are leaders who regard the church as a racing ground. Instead of doing the work or mandate each has been given, and concentrating in doing it with care, they want to zoom off, look into their rear view mirror and come off it with an attitude of carnal satisfaction. When I was a younger Christian, I was told of two pastors from two different churches who were at loggerheads. So much space for two to enjoy under the same big umbrella but one chose to push the other out into the rain. It would not have taken me by surprise if some of their respective leaders had adopted that example. Some leaders, once they start to taste ministry success, they quickly forget their sacred covenant as ministers in the Lord. They make detours from their path of ministry. Sauls who are always suspicious of Davids, and Sauls who are trying to wipe out Davids. Yes, they forget that they are supposed to be in partnership with God, and with the other vine workers in His vineyard. These ministers preach about being members in the same Body but they who are the elbows can't help being envious of the feet because the feet can go places and run fast. They who are the hands pick up an object to poke the eyes.

"I thank my God upon every remembrance of you, always in every prayer of mine making request for you all with joy, for your fellowship in the gospel from the first day until now, being confident of this very thing, that He who has begun a good work in you will complete it until the day of Jesus Christ; just as it is right for me to think this of you all, because I have you in my heart, inasmuch as both in my chains and in the defense and confirmation of the Gospel, you all are partakers with me of grace."

—Philippians 1:3-7.

O Christians, that we be reminded of our being called in the same hope, so we should be working our calling and enjoying it with each other in the same good mind in Him who called. Do not value ourselves to be higher or better in ministry, zoom off, look into our rear view mirror and say to our brethren, "Ha, eat my dust!" God is the One preparing us for the ministry and preparing the ministry to be stewarded by us. Being high-minded about ourselves in it is minusing God from it.

A true story many years ago, Kelly (not her real name) brought her friend and her friend's family into Church. Kelly had asked a few members in the church to make friends with her guests and help make them feel like family. A cell leader's wife, who obviously saw Gail having a good laugh with Kelly's guests, went over afterward and said to Gail, "That family will be taken good care of by our cell group, and that's how it's going to be." That was totally unnecessary. The main purpose in winning souls into God's Kingdom is that they are won over. There should not be fighting about who should be in our cell group or how many more people we have in our group compared to theirs. A good Christian should rejoice in the spiritual prosperity of his brethren, and even help to make the brethren prosper more.

This afternoon, I was at the traffic lights along the highway. I happened to look into my rear view mirror and guess what—the driver in the car behind me was attentively looking downward, like she was typing an important message on her cell phone. When the two cars in front of me started to move, I was so tempted to . . . . naah, I didn't.

*Since the first days of track racing, many deaths have been recorded. If one is not careful, racing can be a very dangerous sport.*

# 6

# It's Really God's Timing!

My friend is fighting cancer. His daughter's wedding has been set for end of the month. There are mixed feelings in the heart of his family and friends. That's about seven hundred thousand, four hundred and ninety six people altogether. Ok, I may be aggrandizing the number but who wouldn't respect and like a guy who is honest in his words and deeds, who is comfortable to be with, and saliently his Christ-like nature to shout about? When you do, you would think that everybody else does too. I have known him and his wife, and their then-toddler since my OM days more than 20 years ago. He has never changed his stance on Jesus and always seeking and after God's heart, showing the way to hundreds . . . . thousands actually, to Christ. The last time my family and I were with him and his wife and giving each other goodbye hugs was the third quarter of last year.

These few months, the wedding guests have been excited, preparing to go to Singapore for their daughter's wedding. He is still so much on the go, being the busy and sough-after itinerant speaker, although he is sometimes slowed down by the illness fatigue and pain. His wife and ministry companion is a huge help during times like this. I have been praying for God's grace and mercy that he is given a chance to walk his daughter down the aisle, and that his only daughter will have her daddy by her side when she walks toward a new chapter in her life. Besides rejoicing with the wedding host family, it may be the last time for many to see my friend.

Many a time, at a juncture like this, when everyone is helpless as to whether there will be an upturn in a situation, even a slight glimpse of a tilt, it gives an impression that the whole spiritual realm is so quiet. Do I dare think? Even if I do, which direction? We want to push things to go our way, what we want, how we want it to be. We think and think, *will God tune His timing to suit our desires?*, and waking up with worn-out minds . . . .

I want to thank God, through the many situations He has allowed me to go through, He has caused me to be more and more in tune to the fact that it is all His timing. It is not wrong for me to pray and talk to Him about it, but His timing is still the best. To top it all, He never fails to care for every detail along the way.

Everything has its time . . . .
Ecclesiastes 3:1-8 says "to everything there is a season, a time for every purpose under heaven:
a time to be born, and a time to die;
a time to plant, and a time to pluck what is planted;
a time to kill, and a time to heal;
a time to break down, and a time to build up;
a time to weep, and a time to laugh;
a time to mourn, and a time to dance;
a time to cast away stones, and a time to gather stones;
a time to embrace, and a time to refrain from embracing;
a time to gain, and a time to lose;
a time to keep, and a time to throw away;
a time to tear, and a time to sew;
a time to keep silence, and a time to speak;
a time to love, and a time to hate;
a time to war, and a time of peace."

I am praying I can slot a meeting up with my friend and his family soon into God's timing.

*What about you? . . . .*

*Have you been waiting upon God for something to happen? I want to encourage you that if it happens or not, and when it happens when it does, you are on the right track—you are waiting upon God. When you do this, you are trusting Him to say what's best for you.*

# 7

# Not In Vain

A special dedication to parents who share the heroic and skillful feat . . . .

School days are here again!
Some sanity we hope to retain
Punctuality we try to attain.

Rising early a problem it ain't
Bad traffic is the driver's disdain
Pumps up blood flow in the vein.

Cars lined up like a train
To see what's up, we need to crane
Such constant woes no good for the brain.

Silly parkers another driver's bane
Confidence in traffic police waned
Everywhere is jammed, even the back lane!

Wouldn't dare think of days with rain
If traffic volume maintains
Traffic standstill can be such pain.

Reaching home . . . . my security and rest fane
A drink, while gazing out the pane
Dreaming of a holiday in Spain . . . .
Coming back to reality, I look at
My children, and I tell myself . . . .
It's worth the pain.

*Someone once said to me, "I'm so glad I don't have to go through all the traffic and waiting in front of schools like you parents. I said, "Pity, you are missing out on a lot."*

# 8

# Go Out

I just spotted a scratch on the back bumper of my 2-month-old car! Someone must have given my car that semi-deep two-inch scratch on the corner when I parked my car somewhere because I did not scratch it. And because the car is only two months old and not at least a few years old, I am feeling kind of upset that my silver MPV is, well, not so perfectly new anymore. I groaned about my scratch woes to my mom. Seeing it from a more practical viewpoint, Mom said I had to accept it as a reality that when we drive around, our car is liable to scratches. Otherwise I had to put my car away in the garage and not drive it at all. But . . . . but Mom, can't it wait till it's at least five years old before getting its first tiny half-inch hairline scratch?

I hear the *sole* reason some parents send their children to Christian home-schooling centers instead of receiving their education in other types of institution is so that their children do not get 'contaminated' by the world's ways of lifestyle. As much as we, as parents, want to protect our children in all areas of their growing up years and shielding them from filth in all aspects, putting or forcing them into an overly sheltered life can bring about an adverse effect on their growth.

Jesus did not tell His disciples to keep to themselves and be secluded from others who are not a part of them. Instead, He said to "go into all the world and preach the Gospel to every creature" (Mark 16:15). Just as Jesus had rebuked the Pharisees and taught them right from wrong (Matthew 23), asked for water from a Samaritan woman (John 4), supped with the tax collectors (Matthew 9) and not to mention calling one to follow Him, He wants us to go out and mix around with the people. We have a call from the Lord to carry out the Great Commission (most familiar version recorded in Matthew 28:16-20) to help others open their eyes toward Jesus. So He actually wants His children to be active *in* the world . . . .

. . . . but not to be *of* the world. Just as our cars are open to scratches on the road, hopefully we will be careful and not go around scratching others. Wherever our children are, not only in school, they are exposed to moral filth. If they receive strong spiritual upbringing with prayer backup always, they need not be easily seen as falling victim to negative worldliness. Instead, they can be His victors in bringing the victims of the world to Jesus.

Sometimes being Christians in the world, we are made to feel like a square peg trying to fit into a round hole. If we know the end of it, we would rather be that peg now than be taken down a peg or two when we meet the Lord. As we go on in life in the world, we may receive some scratches here and there which may mar our otherwise spiritually perfect clean mind. It is up to us really, to either conform or deny, refuse and refrain. We can renew our spirit with God's Word and prayer daily to produce what can be seen on the outward. A renewed heart is the best proof in our representation of our God.

Romans 12:2—"And do not be conformed to this world, but be transformed by the renewing of your mind, that you may prove what is that good and acceptable and perfect will of God."

A spin around town, anyone?

*"Create in me a clean heart, o God, and renew a right spirit within me." Amen!*

Peanut butter scones
Sweetened strawberry jam
Fresh blueberries
Chamomile tea

# 9

# Of Oranges And Apples

Last Sunday was *Chap Goh Meh*, which literally means *15th night* in Chinese Hokkien dialect. It marks the end of a 15-day celebration of the Chinese New Year. In the evening of this day, which is also the Chinese Valentine's Day, we see groups of merry-making people along some of the coastal roads in Penang. Performances by the *Baba-Nyonya* mixed parentage folks are a must, where everyone is dressed in traditional attires.

The highlight of *Chap Goh Meh* is the throwing of oranges by young (and some older ones, depending on previous years' level of success or one's sustainability) maidens into the sea, where bachelors seated in small boats (or Nicholas Cage wannabes showing off in fluorescent g-strings) try to catch those fruits. I am not sure how this match-making game came about decades ago but I know many singles take this Hokkien rhyming phrase *tim kam chuah ho ang* (throw oranges to get a good husband) quite seriously. So seriously that some are said to make an offering or vow in a temple before going for the fruit throwing event with a secret hope that they would do better than the previous years. The organizers eventually created one such fruit throwing event for the guys as well, which promotes the belief of a good wife is in store when one throws apples!

A couple of years ago, I was asking my nearing-40 single friend for gift ideas for my 70-year-old aunt who was getting married. That was Aunt's first marriage to an old friend who was widowed a few years before that. I knew my phone call for gift ideas was in vain when the moment she heard about my aunt, she said *thank You, God, for giving me hope still!* I could feel her doing the jig through the phone.

There are a few reasons why people want to be married. An earthly Christian marriage is a special celebrated bond between a man and a woman and Christ is at the center of it. It is the couple's serious declaration of Christ's love for His church. It should be a lasting commitment, and not something to be abandoned easily. The bible contains verses which encourage marriage; that, one who finds a wife finds a good thing and not only that, but also obtains favor of the LORD (Proverbs 18:22); so do not be an advocate in destroying your union. Hebrews 13:4 reminds married people to hold marriage in high respect as one of God's all. Such sacred union has been in God's plan from the beginning of time, that is why He made man a helper (Genesis 2:18). This is further supported by Ecclesiastes 4:9-11 that two are better than one in terms of helping and lifting up each other, and keeping each other comfortable. This is found to be a true experience to those who have been married for some time already.

On the other hand, we find Paul seriously encouraging the unmarried and the widows to remain single, like he was (1 Corinthians 7:8). I don't think Paul had any bad conception about earthly marriage but he was more concerned about not losing our focus in our service for God. It is true that marriage requires a person to think about the other half, putting food on the table, many things concerning the children, etc., that what is remained in your thinking space, time and energy may not allow you to do the things of God more effectively than how you are doing. That need not be the way. As a couple, when our respective roles in life evolve into having more responsibilities in career and family, we plan so things fit in. We may change ministries and roles in Kingdom service and giving heart to God's ministries and His people should always have a place in our marriage.

In whatever marital status we are in, it will be detrimental to our Christian testimony in God to not do the best we can. If you are single, be content to live your singlehood in Him and serve Him and others, and let your life and your service bring glory to God. If you are married, handling your marriage and household the way God intends can itself speak of your service for Him (1 Corinthians 7:27).

It is perfectly fine to pray and ask God for a life partner even when we are 40 or 50, or even 60 years old . . . . but, chill! It need not have to be a fruity kind of prayer.

*Are you single? Live your life effectively for God.*
*You're married, you say? Live your life effectively for God.*
*You're widowed. Live your live effectively for God.*
*You're divorced? Live your life effectively for God.*

# 10

# A Mother-Daughter Heart

While I was talking with an acquaintance this morning, she told me how she started the business she was doing now. She had acquired the skill from Hong Kong, where she had lived for more than twenty years before coming back for good many months ago. Eve (not her real name) moved to Hong Kong when she married her Hong Kongnese husband. The couple made an agreement that Eve would live in Hong Kong until she was forty, with yearly visits back to Penang to see her family. She did that until a couple of years after her 40th birthday, and months ago she came home. It is now her husband's turn to do most of the travel. What an unselfish and beautiful plan. Eve said she would still return to Hong Kong every now and then to visit her in-laws who have been wonderful to her all these years. Her main reason for coming home for good is her mother.

A woman once said, "If I had carried for nine months and given birth to at least one daughter, let me feel blessed the rest of my life having a daughter. When I am old, let my daughter be the one to see my nakedness, and not another's daughter. Do not take away my integrity as a mother who has a daughter." If a daughter's heart is not carved out to fit into her mother's, the heart bears a devastating picture. I am glad my sister, who is living overseas with her family for the past many years, is making plans for their return to Malaysia soon, as our parents and her in-laws are in their old age. Even if they choose to settle down out of state, my sister can still see our parents many times a year. For the time being, she and our parents talk on the phone every few days, with half-yearly visits.

An elderly woman shares with me how much hurt she harbors. She is 'blessed' with a few daughters, only to bring tears to her during her old age. She pours out her woes to relatives and also in-laws. She says she is not asking much from her daughters but just for them to make trips specially to visit her a few times a year. She claims she has been such a sacrificial mother to them since day one. A 4-hour drive or a 1-hour plane ride to see their mother and stay for a while will make her happy. I cannot answer her few questions as to why situations are such. "I am already nearing 80. Why must I start learning to operate the computer so my daughters can communicate with me through email and I can know what's happening in their lives through Facebook? Why can't they call their mother every few days?"

I am my mother's daughter and I have daughters of my own. I have roles to play on both ends; how I treat my mother and how I am treated by my daughters. The latter I will leave to God's good hands. I am more concerned about how I am welcoming my mother to be a part of my life, my agendas, and what support I can give my mother so she can live her golden years freely. Proverbs 20:20—"Whoever curses his father or his mother, his lamp will be put out in deep darkness" should cause any daughter to step on her brakes and to think. God is not taking lightly at all about a daughter's responsibility toward her mother. He is very serious when His Word talks about the misery of such a daughter—she will not expect any peace. She receives no guidance from Him. When our lamp is snuffed out, how can we see where we are going? Everything comes to a halt in life. There may be no posterity when we are cut off root and branch. Hopeless is she whose lamp is put out in complete darkness!

*Many of us will be familiar with this song written in 1915*
*by Howard Johnson:*
***M** is for the **many** things she gave me*
***O** means only that she's growing **old***
***T** is for the **tears** she shed to save me*
***H** is for her **heart** of purest gold*
***E** is for her **eyes** with love light shining*
***R** means **right** and right she'll always be*

*Put them together, they spell **MOTHER**;*
*a word that means the world to me.*

# 11

# Baby Boom

Aww . . . I just had one of the most gorgeous moments I have not experienced for a long time! I carried a newborn baby in my arms. I visited my friend who has just given birth to her third child. You can say this happy couple and we have some kind of special 'bond'. They have two daughters. Their second daughter and our second daughter share the same first name and half of their Chinese names carry the same character and meaning. Their newborn son and our youngest of three have the same first name and the same sounding half of their Chinese names. Holding little Joshua in my arms that day made me wish I had a couple more babies many years ago.

My favorite pictures depicting the beauty babies bring along with them when they come into the world, are one of a nursing mother and another of a father holding and gazing unspeakable admiration at his baby. In the former, I see newness of life, providence, special attachment, sacrifice and joy. The latter describes strength, tenderness, careful handling, assurance and security. These pictures describe a perfect Father in heaven and our relationship with Him.

God reserves a special place in His heart for babies and children. I guess that is why His Word carries many teachings and reminders about them . . . .

✦ His gift to us—"Behold, children are a heritage from the LORD, the fruit of the womb is a reward." (Psalm 127:3);

✦ Children should not be neglected—"But when Jesus saw it, He was greatly displeased and said to them, 'let the little children come to Me, and do not forbid them; for of such is the Kingdom of God.'" (Mark 10:14);

"'Take heed that you do not despise one of these little ones. For I say to you that in Heaven their angels always see the face of My Father who is in Heaven.'" (Matthew 18:10)

✦ How we should treat children—"Train up a child in the way he should go, and when he is old, he will not depart from it." (Proverbs 22:6);

"And you, fathers, do not provoke your children to wrath, but bring them up in the training and admonition of the Lord." (Ephesians 6:4);

. . . . and many more.

The things that give my heart delightful flutters are when I am watching those little fingers pick something up, when toddlers take the biggest step they can while learning to walk, when babies and little children in little sobs trying to catch their breath after a crying session, when these precious ones laugh uncontrollably at something which only they think is the funniest thing on earth.

We know of a particular baby who is better, greater and different from any other babies in the world. He is the One who is credited to and in control of the many spectacular events that have been happening in the world since He was born. When His earthly parents brought baby Jesus to the temple to do for Him what the custom of the law required, a righteous and devout man Simeon took the baby in his arms and praised God, saying, "Lord, now You are letting Your servant depart in peace, according to Your Word; for my eyes have seen Your salvation which You have prepared before the face of all peoples, a Light to bring revelation to the Gentiles, and the glory of Your people Israel." Such powerful words spoken of the baby Jesus. Also, Anna, a prophetess of a great age, seeing baby Jesus gave thanks to the Lord, and spoke of Him to all those who looked for redemption (Luke 2:21-39). Simeon, whom the Holy Spirit was upon, was waiting to see the baby who was (*and is*) the promised Deliverer of his nation and the Savior of humankind, that when he saw Him, and he knew it was He who had been promised to his nation, he was contented and ready to leave the earth. Simeon knew that with this Baby, hope had come!

*Can you remember the last time you held a baby in your arms, and that special feeling it gave you? Knowing and having He who came to earth as a glorified Baby in your life now is so much more beautiful.*

# 12

# Nest 1/3 Empty

After all the hugs, photos, and our profuse contribution to tissue paper industry, our eldest child walked through the airport departure gate, pulling her trolley bag behind her and her faithful red jacket hanging over her arm. As she walked away from sight, I was nudged into realization that my baby bird has left my nest.

Those of you who read my blog seven years ago about Rebekah, that preteen is now on her own, very cut off from Mom's apron strings. She has set the ball rolling for me and my husband in seeing our children leave home one by one. After giving our children an upbringing in an environment of family closeness, the next couple of days were quite a blur for the four of us. One of us was missing at the dinner table. One of us was not there to do a certain chore at home. I was watering plants and hanging laundry when emotions got the better of me. Tears welled up. I missed my daughter. It takes a parent's heart to know that slight void I am feeling. Separations are never easy for those who appreciate family closeness but certain things need to give way for some other better things to happen.

One thing I am encouraged in our children leaving home is the spiritual environment they have the opportunity to grow up in before they leave the nest. Michael and I are not wonderfully perfect parents but what we know all these years is that what there is to tell our children, it is the Word of God. It is vital that every child born to Christian parents be made ready before he turns the page to a new chapter in his life. This preparation has everything to do with what the Lord wants in a child's life and it begins from the time the child is born. The Bible reminds us in Proverbs 22:6 to "train up a child in the way he should go . . . ."; not in any way our human mind thinks or wants but the way in the knowledge of the Lord.

My prayer is that in every phase of life each of my children is in, his or her heart will always be filled with God's Word; that wherever that child turns, Christian teaching will always be in view.

A couple of days after Rebekah settled into university, she wrote that she had cooked her first meal there. From her explanation, the two dishes sounded exactly like what I cook at home. She is doing her laundry like how she had learnt to at home.

"Therefore you shall lay up these words of mine in your heart and in your soul, and bind them as a sign on your hand, and they shall be as frontlets between your eyes. You shall teach them to your children, speaking of them when you sit in your house, when you walk by the way, when you lie down, and when you rise up."—Deuteronomy 11:18-19.

*Nest 1/3 empty; enjoying the 2/3 full.*

# 13

# A Splendid Thing Called Love

I am a people watcher. I enjoy watching the ways of people while I am waiting at the airport, lazing on the beach or anywhere else where I need to wait without someone to talk to or something to read. Some things I see make me laugh. Just the other day, I was at the mall waiting for the other 2/5 of my family to buy what they needed. There was a very young couple walking arm in arm who, to my guess, were very much in love with each other and they wanted to make it known. Each one wore a side from a pair of something; shoes, socks, dangling earrings. I am ok with the footwear but I would prefer my man not to go around with a dangling earring.

Show of love between two people in a guy-girl relationship sure has evolved much through the times. Finger bands and wrist bands have transmogrified into . . . . dangling earrings? Let's travel back in time to the period where basics are, well, just basics. Whenever I read through the Song Of Solomon, like where I am now in my personal devotion, I can't get used to the fact that love and romance then could be felt with words such as what we read in this book. I imagine myself sitting at a candlelight dinner table for two opposite my (no, he will not be like a gazelle) guy in a restaurant. With heart thumping and all from hints that he is going to say sweet nothings . . . . he opens his mouth and starts describing my hair to be like a flock of goats, my temple he likens to a piece of pomegranate, my neck like a tower built for armoury, and then my teeth look like shorn sheep! Oh wait, he does not miss out that my breasts resemble fawns! I will leave you to imagine my reaction. I think I will settle for a simple *shall we share a bowl of creme brûlée?*

I have nothing against Hebrew poetries. It could be that a woman with forehead sides like a piece of fruit and an arsenal-like neck caused a testosterone rush in those days. Christians suggest that Song Of Solomon is an analogy to God's love for His people. The dramatic description of her boyfriend to her friends by the Shulamite woman tells us she is so much in love with him and she knows his love for her is great too. He sounds like a perfect man. Basically, the Song Of Songs is glorifying God, making aware of His marvellous creation and celebrating His gift between man and woman; the gift called love. This gift demonstrates the significance God puts on love and commitment.

I was surprised with a marriage proposal from my then-boyfriend in quite an unexpected way. We were cruising at 30,000 feet above sea level when he, almost like what they do in magic shows, whipped out a diamond solitaire set in gold. That boyfriend later became husband. Depending on which phase of life one is at, that spunky act could be seen as "aww . . . . how romantic (scream . . . sigh . . . swoon)", or "he's good; doing it at 30,000 feet above sea level, there's no escape for the girl!"

There can be so many creative ways in showing another person our love for him or her. Some love stay. Some, sadly do not. There is one love shown to us that is so great that nothing can take its place—God's love through His Son! Paul aptly said it in Romans 8:38-39, "For I am persuaded that neither death nor life, nor angel nor principalities nor power, nor things present nor things to come, nor height nor depth, nor any other created thing, shall be able to separate us from the love of God which is in Christ Jesus our Lord." Amen!

I was driving my son home from school when we were talking about girls. I asked him what he would write to a girl if he liked her. From the back seat, hungry and tired from school activities, he mumbled he would write her a poem:

hey,
i'm not gay;
see you this thursday,
in Queensbay.

This boy has hope yet, I'm telling you.

*What's your love story?*

# 14

# Knock! Knock!

I said to my friend who had just given birth that I would be visiting her soon, in between guests. She wished me happy hosting when I joked that I might be opening a hotel. Staying guests in my house usually come in intervals of a few months. This time round, from now for six weeks, I am welcoming and hosting four sets of guests. I will be laundering the guest room bedding more often than ever before. It is quite common for us to clean a bit more here and there when we have guests stay over. I cannot imagine having my guests stay in a dusty room, their backs itching from bed bug bites and showering in a mold-infested bathroom!

Scenario One: You are not yet a Christian. The door bell rings. You open the door and to your surprise, it is Jesus! He introduces Himself, you think it is some kind of a joke. You think it is Jim Caviezel under good makeup. After talking with your Guest who is still standing outside your door, you are convinced that He is indeed Jesus Christ; a name you have heard a few times from your friends, and now He is standing outside your door. Will you let Him in?

Scenario Two: You are a Christian. One day while you are going about doing your own things in your own home, the door bell rings. You look through the peep hole and you recognise it is Jesus! Are you going to be so excited that you open the door at once or are you going to panic? You cannot open your door for Him to enter your house because you need to clear some things first from your CD collection and magazine rack to lock them up in the storeroom.

In Scenario One, the door is the door of your heart. This Guest is not coming in to stay for three days, leave you with soiled bed linens and towels, and then leave. Once you open that door, He will come in to stay forever. Not only that, He is coming in with a gift—Eternal Life! He promises you an unceasing intimate fellowship which He reserves just for you. The second scenario talks about Christians who make up the church. He does not want us to be lukewarm in our walk with Him, which can be seen in our works. He does not want us to forget what He had done for us so we would not be shamed in nakedness. In some churches today, Jesus is not welcome. They have detoured and become organizations of performance and institutions of achievements. Nevertheless,

He still loves us and wants to give us another chance (Revelation 3:14-22).

Revelation 3:20—"Behold, I stand at the door and knock. If anyone hears my voice and opens the door, I will come in to him and dine with him, and he with Me."

*"Knock! Knock!"*
*"Who's there?"*
*"Jesus!"*
*"Jesus who?"*
*"Jesus, the Christ . . . . and it's not a joke."*

# 15

# Boys To Men

Yesterday, out of the blue, my soon-to-be teenager son asked, "Mom, what if I keep a mustache?" That caught me by surprise while I was driving. It also reminded me of other behaviors, preferences and the way he discusses things with me which I noticed have changed in Josh the past many months. "So Mom, what do you think of me with a mustache?" I answered, "I'm sure you will be very handsome." His two elder sisters thought that was cute. My son, who is slowly inching into adolescence is looking at things from a different perspective now. That could only mean one thing—my baby will soon come out of his boyhood caterpillar into the cocoon of adolescence, and it is only less than ten years before he is a full butterfly into his manhood years. Huge wow! Only a mom will know what this feels like. I guess when Josh is 18, I will be calling out to fellow-moms, "I need a hug!"

This is suddenly happening so fast. I have been reading *That's My Teenage Son* by Rick Johnson, a book which I strongly recommend to parents, youth and young adult workers, and mothers of much older sons . . . . even wives! It helps us to understand so much more about how the different areas in a male work. There are some pretty interesting points shared by the author, who is also the founder of *Better Dads* ministry which focuses on equipping parents in bringing up boys. The book explained logically the reasons why a male behaves how he does and links this to a few areas that influence such behaviours including the people that that male grew up with, such as the type of women and male role models. One particular area which the author talks about that I find insightful is on 'healthy masculinity', and he does not mean a well worked out v-shape body with biceps tearing at the sleeves . . . . although that physicality may work well to enhance the good that is going on inside, i'm sure. Watching the ways of other boys and men has been like a case study for me as I read this book and I must admit that I appreciate the author's factual reasoning based on God's plan in each man.

Although there is a large supply of materials, seminars, camps and whatever we can think of to guide parents in bringing up children, I, as a mother to my son, know that looking to God in this is of paramount importance. I choose to trust Him to lead, protect, and provide for my son Josh, I hold on to His many promises on the blessing in having children. I hope that at the different stages in my son's life I can rejoice in the fact that blessed is she who bore and nursed him.

I realize that in not so many years more, Josh will leave home to face the outside world. Just as Rick Johnson suggests about male mentors, I pray that God will bring along many great male Christian mentors into my son's life, that Josh will be able to learn from them the meaning of healthy masculinity.

Psalm 127:3-5: "Behold, children are indeed a heritage from the LORD, the fruit of the womb is a reward. Like arrows in the hand of a warrior, so are the children of one's youth. Happy is the man who has his quiver full of them; they shall not be ashamed, but shall speak with their enemies in the gate."

then Josh continued, "Do you think I should just keep a line of mustache or grow a whole lot of beard?" Hmm . . .

*Dad, when was the last time you played football, swam, watched a movie, built with Lego, washed the car, discussed about school, talked about God, etc . . . . with your son?*

# 16

# Bananas Don't Split

I have never felt so lonely in any of my children's schools as I did a few days ago in my son's new high school. I attended the orientation briefing for new students which was conducted solely in Mandarin. A 'banana' (its colors resembling a Chinese with limited ability in things Chinese, with Western tendencies) like I am, oh, how I suffered intellectually and emotionally as the minute hand on the watch did not seem to move. The 2-hour orientation seemed like forever. To make matters worse, there was a caucasian lady beside me who was there for her daughter who was seated in the front half of the hall with the other students, while the lady's younger child was beside her translating the briefing for her to English. Now, an egg (color resemblance thingy again—go figure) is not something a banana finds fun having around during moments like this. By this time, I felt really tiny and more lost.

It was a classic experience of confusion of tongues like during the building of the Tower of Babel, I believe. After all, I do feel distant from the Chinese who tend to rattle away in Mandarin with each other even when there are non-Mandarin speaking folks of other races in the conversation. I normally feel embarrassed of their insensitivity and 'scattered' from them. When my husband and I decided to enrol Josh into the Chinese-based school for the Cambridge studies in its international studies section, we knew there would be a reasonable mount of language barrier for us but I was not prepared for such great measure of hindrance since there were also many students from other parts of the world enrolled in the school. If we do the opposite from what was being briefed during the orientation, will we be penalized?

Maybe I should hold the people during Noah's time responsible for this language problem. After the flood, nations were descended from Noah, branching off through his sons Shem, Ham and Japheth. God's plan was for mankind to form many nations and peoples. Things were going quite well when a bunch of guys decided to take things into their own hands so as to protect their togetherness. So in disregard of the Almighty's will, their work began—making of bricks, building of a city and a tower whose top would reach the heavens, and making a name for themselves. This ill-mannered attitude caused the LORD to come down to see all that the sons of men were up to. He was not pleased at all. At His very word, the people suddenly spoke in different languages, that they could not understand one another's speech. How would they continue to still plan and work together if they could not understand each other? At the end of the day, they were scattered all over the face of the earth (Genesis 11:1-9).

These people learnt, a bit late, that God would frustrate every proud man's ventures that purposefully turned themselves against Him. In this setting, bewilderment set in, they lost their union with each other, the Lord's hand was out against them, and of course, their plans came to naught. For whose heart, if hardened against Him, can prosper?

I know I am going to take this language barrier as a challenge upon myself, for what will I gain if I give up? A challenge in knowing more Mandarin than just limited words and phrases here and there; a challenge in helping those on the other side of the fence to see things with a more wide-angled lense. When the orientation meeting was dismissed, I had a good few words with the principal to further understand what was expected of my son and his parents, and to share some useful suggestions. After that, I made friends with six other banana moms, and like what they say, *bananas of the world unite!*

*Do not upset God's plan for the sake of our own.*

Bacon and parmesan scones
Fresh or dried cranberries
Lemon verbena tea

# 17

# Factuality In Honesty

I received news from a shop I have been buying things from. On such date to such date 'everything is on sale', the message announced. Since supplies at home were running low, and I could get whatever I bought at a lower than usual price, it was a good idea to hit the store. I went in and took what I wanted. As I was paying, I saw that a few of the things I took were rung up at normal price. I reminded the cashier about the message stating that everything was on sale. She said it meant that everything in the shop had to be sold off. What?! I said, then, the message should have read 'everything is *for* sale'. I felt cheated.

Three days later, my daughter and I spotted a sign at a shop selling trinkets—'3 free 1'. What do we have to do with the three in order to get one for free? Will we get into trouble if we steal three, or given one free for stealing? What about 'break three free one', or 'use three free one'? Signs or business news like these should convey clear information so that innocent folks will not misunderstand, be misled or feel cheated in any way . . . . or they will just walk off the same way they walked in—not buying anything—and most likely will not come back again.

How do we convey the Gospel to another person? Do we communicate salvation in Jesus with all spiritual magniloquence? An idea that is so high-flown that will make the listener want to believe in Jesus so much . . . . only for half-right reasons. We share about the appealing benefits of asking Jesus to be our Savior but purposely leave out the other parts of having Jesus in our lives—submission to His Lordship, discarding of certain old lifestyle, and later on, possible rejection or persecution from unbelieving family members and friends. Someone taught me before to 'just catch them first'. If we do that, it is only half truth that we are sharing.

A lady (let's call her Emily) was having a host of problems including a stubborn illness. She was approached by a Christian who promised her a sure-cure the moment she accepted Jesus as her personal Lord and Savior. Emily was very excited that finally things were beginning to go right for her. She said the sinner's prayer. A few weeks later, everything was still the same old for Emily. She was looking forward so much to the 'promise' uttered by the Christian who led her in the sinner's prayer. We believe that there were and are so many miracles done by our Lord. I have also heard umpteen testimonies today of instant healing happening at the moment of prayer. Our God is a God who heals, and He does what He wills.

Emily slowly let go of her new life in Christ and slid back to the old. About two years after that, Emily met another Christian lady who told her about Christ, and offered to pray for her. The moment she heard that name, she cringed away in fear of being victim again to another, which she called, 'con job'. Emily later thanked this lady for her perseverance in pursuing her, being Emily's friend first and gained her trust, and shared her own real life experience with Emily. For through this, Emily recommitted her life to Christ, this time for real. The lady guided Emily through a series of new life study where Emily began to feel whole again. And guess what? Illness was such a big *'h'* word for Emily already. H for history, and H definitely for Hallelujah! Today, Emily is cut off from her mentor's apron strings. She is now reaching out to others, and only going back to her mentor for bits of advice and fellowship.

Failure to convey clear and correct information about our faith can happen in different ways. May God give us wisdom. John

8:32—"And you (*they*) shall know the truth, and the truth shall make you (*them*) free."

*How about this . . . .*
*Whenever people walk in, let them walk out with Jesus.*

# 18

# Let It Flow

". . . . you shall be like a watered garden, and like a spring of water, whose waters do not fail."

—Isaiah 58:11

It was already more than three hours since the water cut and oil and gravy on my wok, pots, crockery, utensils, cutlery and stove were drying up. Thank God my friend who lived two streets away agreed to let me do my washing in her home. As I was packing the plates into the back of my car, my 4-year-old neighbor asked, "Aunty Gina, what are you doing?" I replied, "There's no water supply in my house so I'm taking the dishes down to the river to wash." Nicol gave me an ok-i-believe-you look. I do not usually bluff children this way but it was late and I was tired; a little harmless sarcasm to retain some sanity, why not?

There was some work that needed to be done to the pipes on my street which apparently would not take long. The management thought it was not necessary to send a notice to the home owners since it would be done in a jiffy. We made two complaints about our kitchen taps being still dry, they went to check, and found out that the guy who was responsible for turning the water back on, like two hours before that, had forgotten all about it. A slight negligence that brought much inconvenience to many people. After water supply resumed, our taps had to be turned on for a long time before we saw clean water again.

If we have been a believer for some time, knowing that we have been found in the Lord and enjoying a spiritual relationship with Him, would we dare think of what it would be like if we were cut off from Him totally? Jesus calls Himself the source of Living Water. He promises that at conversion, every believer receives an exceedingly abundant flow of God's grace. Grace so full that any volume of sin we carry over He quashes effortlessly. He shows that the water of Jacob's well, normal physical water (John 4:13-15) brings about a very short satisfaction. But it will be different when we come to Him and drink of His kind of water, the grace that comes only from the Spirit of God. This Water shall be in us a well of water, springing up into everlasting life. As long as we are connected to Him, this Water will not stop flowing so we will not thirst. There is no lack or dissatisfaction.

As we live in this life of everflowing spiritual refreshment, being cleansed and purified, we are also living a life of spiritual rest in Christ. By Him, we are made to increase in spiritual things. The obvious distinction between His people and the people of the world will be pointless for any simple comparison. Since this is so, and we are tasting the satisfaction of His fountain of water springing up into everlasting life, would we actually dare live a minute cut off from Him?

Complacency, giving in to temptations, and other sins can slowly dry up our spiritual taps. The problems that come with drying taps and the pain in trying to carry on living a parched life are too much to bear. I don't think I would dare imagine being cut off from Jesus.

Our water did not completely clear up until the next day.

*In a life of easy excess to water, it is so inconvenient to have a water cut. In a life of direct excess to the Living Water, it is so frightening to even think of being cut off from Him.*

# 19

# Be Thankful And Give Thanks Always

Thankfulness is a multi-blessing thing. Being thankful brings about a spirit of joy from an attitude of gratefulness. It also draws people and even more blessings to us. Being thankful makes us want to give because we are always overflowing to the brim. Health reports tell that a thankful attitude allows the human body to ooze out the good juices which strengthen our cells and hormones, and slows down aging. Thankfulness brings about peace. "Now Godliness and contentment is great gain."

—1 Timothy 6:6.

Having gone through nearly half a century in life by the loving grace of my God, I am thankful for all that I was allowed to be and do. I had a few regrets which became mere shadows in all the God-given achievements. Nothing comes near to the joy of knowing that each success I experienced, it was done so with Him. For what God has been and given to this vessel, I pray I will always be worthy to say that "I press toward the goal for the prize of the upward call of God in Christ Jesus."

—Philippians 3:14.

All the wonders of the world do not have much worth when compared to each soul saved into the Kingdom of God. I am so thankful for the many lives I have had the chance to witness crossing over from darkness to Light, watching how condemned lives changed to lives of favor and triumph in the Lord. I pray I will continue to see such miracles. Through them my faith is also strengthened further knowing that the God I worship is a true and living God. "Likewise, I say to you, there is joy in the presence of the angels of God over one sinner who repents."

—Luke 15:10.

No matter our age, everyone likes to be appreciated. Appreciation signifies being shown the full worth of what we are to the other person and what we do for him or her. But being the one appreciating and saying *thank you* carries a bigger worth. It takes a humble heart to recognize having to say *thank you*. A humble heart is blessed by God. Showing our appreciation to someone also shows we are not taking the other person for granted. However, there is a thin line between 'to be thankful' and 'to give thanks'. We are being thankful when we are filled with gratitude; it comes from how we feel inside us. We feel touched because something good was said to us or done for us. God wants us to give thanks in everything, which includes not only the good but also the undesirable things which may come our way. When we do so, we are trusting Him that He will take all these to work together for our good, fulfilling His purpose in making us to become more Christ-like. "In everything give thanks: for this is the will of God in Christ Jesus for you."

—1 Thessalonians 5:18.

Keeping a spirit of thankfulness and showing my gratitude to people around me is what I desire to do. This, in itself, is a testimony as a Christian. I used to sometimes forget to utter a word of thanks, not because I was not grateful but I was so touched that my eyes were fixed on the gift for some time or my mind was processing the kind words said to me over and over again that I just had not reached the saying *thank you* part yet. But I must say I am doing much better these days— say *thank you* first and do the eyes and mind part later! "Every good gift and every perfect gift is from above, and comes down from the Father of lights, with whom there is no variation or shadow of turning."

—James 1:17-18.

Special *thank you* and praise be to God for blessing me with a home and family. My parents gave me what is aptly called 'family' while I was growing up. Having people to hold and to love, and knowing that I am also being loved make good remedy for the end of a tiring day. Occasionally I see or hear of a family with harmful dysfunctionality. This is sad because in such a situation there is always a person or a couple of people in the family who think of spreading the harm. Why do it in the first place? And to your own flesh and blood?! I also thank God for my friends, like you, for what is life outside home if we do not have friends? My few 40-something-year-old friendships I cherish dearly. I learnt much about friendships from my parents while growing up, but the greatest and perfect friendship I received from Jesus. He said, "Greater love has no man than this, than to lay down one's life for his friends. You are My friends if you do whatever I command you . . . . I have called you friends, for all things that I heard from My Father I have made known to you."

—John 15:13,15b.

*Blessed Thanksgiving!*

# 20

# The Land Of Dried Abalone
# And Dried Scallop

There are a few things in which I marvel at Kowloon, Hong Kong. The last time I visited her was about twenty years ago. In the city, there were masses of concrete in the air. Vehicles were filling the air with exhaust fumes while people were doing that by smoking their lungs out. Today, I see not an improvement in the air, but instead it is even more glutted with modern development and impurities.

*Chou san. Lei ho?* And that is about all the Cantonese you will get from me for now. I am writing this from my 6th floor room overlooking the courtyard in the Sheraton Kowloon. Mike is here for his summit and when he asked if I would like to come along, I jumped at the chance for a break from busy schedules. Also, since I had not set foot on this land for two decades, I thought it would be a swell idea to visit again. But now that I am here, I feel lost. There is not really any work for me to do here. I have all the time I want and people serve me. Coming from 100 degrees Fahrenheit or so, this early spring temperature triggers my happy senses!

The courtyard is lined with very healthy rich green palms of different species and some colourful flowering plants. A serene and welcoming sight to the eyes, this view tells a totally opposite story to what is going on the moment one steps out of the hotel. As soon as the heavy doors swing open, you get a half-and-half of a din of all kinds of noise and the choking smell of polluted air. In the shops, milk powder is double the price back home. Some other things carry lavish price tags too. I remember how much more affordable it was to shop here, but today, it looks like the earning and spending lifestyle in Hong Kong has shot past the normal inflation ratio I am used to. I see the phone and tablet technology has taken over much of life here. By the roadsides, in the trains, in cafes, and about just anywhere else people are looking toward one direction—downward—into their phone or tablet. Some people do not chat in eateries, but each person watches a part of a movie in his own tablet. When they finish eating, they leave, and probably continue on the movie during their next meal. In the restaurant where we ate yesterday, there were five friends having dinner together. With half eaten food in front of them, each person had a phone in his or her hand. They were talking . . . . about their phones. This went on for a long time.

Anywhere in the world, being modern and advanced in technology usually gives an impression of success. It can be frightening in some cases especially where I hear of church leadership meetings being held on internet chat. There is no need for the group to meet in person. After all, God has given us technology, they argue. I say, come on, you can do better than that in making stories. Or what about making it a norm 'going to church' by watching a church service program on the TV week after week for an abled person? Like I said, it is 'anywhere *in the world*' . . . . just in the world . . . . because it is all part of the world's way of understanding life. No person or source knows about life more than the one true and living God. He is life and He created life. Looking at the extensive achievement into modernity and a high dependance on it, like in Hong Kong, I am thinking how her spiritual side is like in the past decades. Has it been a good steady climb too? Everything else is on the rise here. What about her people's choice of real life— eternal life?

Taken from an excerpt in Deuteronomy 30, I bless the people of Hong Kong with this: "Choose life, that both you and your descendants may live; that you may love the Lord, that you may obey His voice, and that you may cling to Him, for He is your life and the length of your days." Amen!

*May you be filled with God's love which overflows to the other nations around you.*

# 21

# God Knows My Name

Tomorrow my daughter is going to school dressed in a beach hat, hello kitty sunnies, a scarf and a Mongolian robe . . . . just so that she will not be recognized. She came home grousing about how so often her name was called each time the teacher wanted to give an example in a lesson or to get a student to help with some work. Today three teachers were calling her name for just anything. So, she said, she had to answer to almost ten times of *Hannah Loh*. Her Physics teacher, who happened to be my Physics and Add Math teacher, introduced Hannah to the class as her 'granddaughter'. She said that since she had taught Hannah's mom before, and Hannah was the next generation, 'granddaughter' would be fitting.

Remember the sitcom *Cheers*, with the theme song *Everybody Knows Your Name*? Well, I think Hannah is feeling quite like that now. But I shared my two cents' worth with her, that in many situations, having her name called frequently might not mean anything bad or unpleasant. It could mean that she is much in the caller's favor or that she is a good worker in that particular assignment that needed to be done. It could also help her stay awake in class! Hannah humphed . . . .

Today I know I belong to God and He knows my name because He said so in His Word. He has chosen me to be His spiritual Israel. I am His workmanship created and constructed in Christ for His glory. This firm promise is an antitoxin to Satan's poison. What a reassurance that makes me fully aware of being sealed in God's promise. A promise of many unfathomable mysteries yet so penetrable into my heart. All these because He has called me by my name, the name He would call people who are known as God's people. Isaiah 43:1-2 notes, "But now, thus says the LORD, who created you, o Jacob, and He who formed you, o Israel: 'Fear not, for I have redeemed you; I have called you by your name; you are Mine. When you pass through the waters, I will be with you; and through the rivers, they shall not overflow you. When you walk through the fire, you shall not be burned, nor shall the flame scorch you.'"

After calling me to Him, out from the world, He continues to make sure that I am always in good hands. He cares for me and feeds me from His Word. His affection for me knows no bounds for He compares His intimacy with me as one where He would lay down His life for me. John 10:3-4, 14-15—"To Him the doorkeeper opens, and the sheep hear His voice; and He calls His own sheep by name and leads them out. And when He brings out His own sheep, He goes before them; and the sheep follow Him, for they know His voice . . . . 'I am the good shepherd; and I know My sheep, and am known by My own. As the Father knows Me, even so I know the Father; and I lay down My life for the sheep.'"

Besides the spiritual call from the Holy Spirit, the Bible also recorded God's verbalized calling to His children in some occasions. Exodus 3:4—"So when the LORD saw that he turned aside to look, God called to him from the midst of the bush and said, 'Moses, Moses!' And he said, 'Here I am.'" God called out to a young child in 1 Samuel 3. Because Samuel was young and had no experience in hearing God's call, it was at the third time of calling that he knew God was calling him. "Now the LORD came and stood and called as at other times, 'Samuel! Samuel!' And Samuel answered, 'Speak, for Your servant hears.'" (verse 10). Jesus called out to a tax collector, someone who was considered spiritually sinful at that time. Luke 19:5—"And when Jesus came to the place, He looked up and saw him, and said to him, 'Zachaeus, make haste and come down, for today I must stay at your house.'" Jesus called out to a man who would do anything to prove that God was his number one enemy—Saul! Acts 9:3-7—"As he (Saul) journeyed he came near Damascus, and suddenly a light shone around him from Heaven. Then he fell to the ground, and heard a voice saying to him, 'Saul, Saul, why are you persecuting Me?' And he said, 'Who are You, Lord?' Then the Lord said, 'I am Jesus, whom you are persecuting . . . .' . . . . And the men who journeyed with him stood speechless, hearing a voice but seeing no one."

*Today, when you hear God's call, do not wait. No matter how young or old you are, or you could be a modern day Saul, do not dismiss or reject God's call. Answer* **here I am!**

*Cheers, God knows your name!*

# 22

# The Name's Christ . . . . Jesus Christ!

James Bond is back; now a new movie called Skyfall. Advertisements are everywhere informing of its coming soon and calling on people to go and watch. Last week, local radio stations gave away free passes to the movie's screening to callers who could answer a simple question. Looking at how straightforward the questions were served to tell how athirst the cinemas were for the listeners to win and go for the screening. After decades of the world watching a suave-looking hero in a suit with a propensity for having sophisticated gadgets and sexy women within his reach, does a next James Bond movie still have a power to draw a huge audience? As far as I know about James Bond movies, it's usually a guy in a tux with unique mastery over some specially built gadgets promising sure-win results. Then after a day's work, he comes back to rest only to find a bombshell waiting when he opens his bedroom door or closet, and for all we know, the larder too. I have never had an interest, and still cannot find myself to, in any James Bond movie. No way, Jose, it is all too quasi-thrilling for me. I would go and watch Jack Sparrow or Thor anytime, ha!

My daughter is more realistic. Her hero is David, son of Jesse (1 Samuel 16). She admires David not because the Bible says he was good-looking (verse 12). She likes the way David handled the many different situations he was caught in, and even more so because he was after God's own heart. David was not perfect but the beauty of his heart shone through and passed his imperfections.

I vote for Queen Esther and the Apostle Paul (Acts 9). They reflect my appreciation for resourcefulness, insightful capacity, steadfastness and selflessness. They would make shrewd and honest business people.

Many Christians put heroic labels on leaders, mentors and preachers they admire. In some cases, they do this unmindful of their misjudgment. By doing so, they put themselves in a position where they may be led off course in their faith; believing something to be true when it is not, and avoiding the truth when it should be followed. When we look at what is on the surface, thinking that it is cool to follow, so we follow, and like what they say, the rest is history. Well, look out, the rest may be history forever. In these times, there is a good deal of folks who pretend to the Spirit. I am not against preachers as debonair as Cary Grant but we just do not follow unthinkingly. Take notice of 1 John 4:1 alerting believers to not believe every spirit, to test the spirits, to see if they are of God because many false prophets have gone out into the world to deceive the unsuspecting and steal believers out of believing what is true. Christians who are familiar with the Word will have instinctual tendencies to check it out (Acts 17:11), and with the Holy Spirit's guidance, be able to perceive doctrines which are contradicting to that of God's.

We cannot blindly leave our spiritual food intake in the hands of any preacher or teacher who comes our way. A theology degree, a confident and fluent speaker, a clerical collar or robe, and a good ministry writeup mean nothing if Jesus is not preached and preached according to the Scriptures. If one claims to believe that God is the Gospel, why should one bring forth preaching on other things besides God?

*One effective way to make heroes popular and keep coming back is the encouraging response from the audience. Think about it . . . .*

# 23

# Borrowed Authority

I stopped what I was doing to wait for a monster to appear from inside my neighbour's house. I was tending to my plants at the front of my house in the afternoon and my neighbor and her family were leaving their house. Their 4-year-old was throwing tantrums because she wanted to stay home, and irritation was mounting as the adults were trying unsuccessfully to persuade the little one to get into the car. Suddenly Grandma's bulb lit up, and she called out to her grandchild, "If you don't come now, a monster will come out of the house." Seeing that the child was adamant that she was not going with them, I was excited that I was going to see a real monster appear. Imagine my disappointment and a sense of victory in the child when there was no monster.

My aunt used to have an uncanny habit of mentioning my name to her grandchildren so they would behave. She would first verbally paint a terrifying picture of me having disquieting strictness on misbehaving children, being the *tua kor* (eldest aunt on father's side). Grownups now, the children have adopted a rather 'careful' way when talking to me. An act of sheer idiocy but that is what fake or borrowed authority is!

Christian leaders too, know how to 'borrow' authority, and use it to their own pleasure and gain. Young and unsuspecting believers make perfect victims. This is how it normally goes: a series of sermons on God's anointed (the popular passage being 1 Samuel 24 where David spared Saul's life) and how we ought not to 'touch' them; a list of Bible verses on the consequence of disobeying leadership; and then, a list of Bible verses on the blessings that come with obeying leadership. While there is absolute truth in all Scripture about obedience toward authority, there is no way God had said anything about leaders being always right and they can do whatever their human minds think is right and no wrong can be seen in leaders. Leaders cannot borrow authority by plucking any verse they like out of the Bible and use it as a weapon of prevention in their ministry; preventing any church member from spoiling their plans. A real leader will lead with humble authority; he will lead with a firm foundation in God and His grace; he will lead like Jesus. On the congregation's side, obedience is the correct way to go if it is done on the grounds of Truth. We should not blindly give firm allegiance only to find, one day, that we have given our commitment to something fake. In fact, "He who justifies the wicked, and he who condemns the just, both of them alike are an abomination to the LORD." (Proverbs 17:15).

Sadly, not many Christians escape the sinful control of borrowed authority; the main factor being fear. It is not common to breathe in Church today without being choked by the impurity of borrowed authority. Some leaders tend to equate church leadership to self power, and they make sure the congregation know it is *the* way to go. These leaders have made the Christian Church to look like an institution for those who either can still think for themselves and make up their own minds from profound evidences in the Bible, or be led astray.

Christians, let's look to neither philosophy nor legalism, but let's set our eyes and mind and heart to Christ only. "As you therefore have received Christ Jesus the Lord, so walk in Him, rooted and built up in Him and established in the faith, as you have been taught, abounding in it with thanksgiving. Beware lest anyone cheat you through philosophy and empty deceit, according to the tradition of men, according to the basic principles of the world, and not according to Christ. For in Him dwells all the fullness of the Godhead bodily; and you are complete in Him, who is the head of all principality and power." (Colossians 2:6-10).

*Cowardice aside, let the children know who the real authority is!*

# 24

# Merdeka!

Despite the heat and humidity (not my cup of tea for a holiday), I enjoyed myself with my family at the Merdeka (Independence) parade in the Esplanade. My daughter's high school choir, the defending champ this year in the state of Penang, was invited to perform, which you could have guessed our main reason for being there. After the inspection of guards by our State Governor, the choir opened the performance-cum-parade with two songs. The parade was colorful and the people were happy. I saw Penangnites of different races clustered along the road on both sides. Contingents representing government departments, school uniform bodies, bands, non-governmental bodies, etc., all smartly and creatively decked out in their Merdeka best; one by one marched past eager spectators, putting up some sort of staging when they passed the grand stands.

All the marching groups looked splendid but some caught my eye more than others. Bands from various Chinese schools placed at different stretches in the parade brightened up the atmosphere. Each time as the line was getting quiet, another band could be heard closing in with an upbeat patriotic song. Oh, such gaiety! I have always enjoyed watching Chinese school bands. Not only for the fact that I have been brought up to appreciate good music, but also their band discipline— the way they march on a straight line while playing music in harmony, sometimes having to keep a 90-degree head turn too! The baton-twirling drum major in a precisely military bearing I should not miss mentioning adds to the pageantry of a great band.

This morning I also saw an active part of our local telecommunication service provider Telekom Malaysia. The public listed company gave an enthusiastic display in their march. I am sure many present who detected their gung-ho-ness wished the same intensity would come out of their telecom lineworks.

My other favorite was the few biking groups, where the convoy gave a thrilling climax to the parade.

A lover of mid spring and early fall weather, I must say that the Merdeka parade was worth my 2.5 hours of sweating (and not to mention an aching arm from video-taking!). I'm proud of you, Penang. A well put up show with no arrogantly domineering pomp to show off and excessive money spent, I saw wisdom in the management. Merdeka! Merdeka! Merdeka!

One day . . . . soon, you and I will be part of a magnificent happening; so magnificently majestic and glorious that it is going to make any best parade we have ever seen seem so insignificant. The Apostle Paul's first letter to the Thessalonians (4:16-17) gives an appropriate description: "For the Lord Himself will descend from Heaven with a shout, with the voice of an archangel, and with the trumpet of God. And the dead will rise first. Then we who are alive and remain shall be caught up together with them in the clouds to meet the Lord in the air. And thus we shall *always* be with the Lord." Amen!

*Let's put on our merdeka best, today, and always . . . . for we are already in the joyous and triumphant parade!*

Plain American scones
Clotted cream
Mixed berries jam
Chocolate-coated Acaiberries
Lavender tea

# 25

# Little Children, Come!

After a 5-year hiatus in anything children, ministry-wise— preparing lessons, buying glitter blue and construction papers, making the children laugh, making some cry, and imparting spiritual morals to delicate lives—I mustered just the grit I needed to step into Children's Church last Sunday. The all too familiar atmosphere of noise, music, chatter, laughter all bundled into one hit me like one opening the door to a windy day outside—whoosh. I was caught off balanced and disorientated for a bit. My mind immediately shifted to lavender-lined pathways in a countryside. Then I wished I had a wand to change everyone into cute little cuddly puppies.

Meeting familiar faces of old friends and new friends helped ease the confusion eventually. A couple of minutes into songs, I was doing some 'walk walk walk walk in the Light, walk walk walk walk in the Light . . . .' with the children. For the last part, I was assigned to a class of a dozen big boys and girls. It was pretty different from what I was used to— fifteen children of toddlers to preteens. I sat in the class to see what was to be done with the children. I made friends with some of them and was especially drawn to an exceptionally quiet boy. We became friends . . . .

I prayed about this for a few weeks. I finally decided to visit the Children's Church because of a few reasons. I also saw the need of the little ones to be guided to walk walk walk walk in the Light. Children are a people close to the heart of our Lord. He uses children as a perfect focus on how Christians should be made to parallel a child's belief without great effort if Christians were to enter the Kingdom of Heaven. I put myself in Matthew 19:13-15. Parents were bringing their children to Jesus; some probably seeking for healing while some could not wait for His hands to just touch their precious ones. The disciples saw this as a hindrance to Jesus' ministry work and a slowdown in His journey. In annoyance, they started to rebuke the children. We are relieved that Jesus had more love than all his disciples combined, and put a stop to that when He said, "let the little children come to Me, and do not forbid them . . . ." (verse 14).

Christian parents should bring their children to Jesus. They should not hide their little ones from knowing Jesus. When parents bring their children to Children's Church, they are bringing them with hope and belief that their children will be embraced and blessed by Jesus. Hindering these children does not mean by merely pushing them out of the Children's Church door. The children in Children's Church should be treated as how Christ would the children. Therefore, words and actions by the teachers may make or break the children's understanding of Jesus' passion and love for them. How they are being welcomed, spoken with, taught, disciplined, noticed, persuaded and encouraged can determine if these are done with sincere love for them. The children will bring this *love* (or not) with them into their adolescent and adult years.

Matthew 18:10—"Take heed that you do not despise one of these little ones, for I say to you that in heaven their angels always see the face of My Father who is in Heaven." Can you hear the protective tone of concern from Jesus when He said this? Although when Jesus said 'little ones', it could be that He did not only directly mean little children, but He was also looking toward describing those who were weak, obscure and did not know where to go or how to look after themselves properly. I would like to think that children are indeed not too different from that.

*Look back to your own childhood. Will you describe it as good or bad? Why?*

# 26

# Wouldn't Exchange The Ten Hours For Anything

**M**y husband Michael wished he had heeded my advice much earlier when he did what looked like the 20th dash for the toilet in less than a day! He could not hold in any food or liquid even in very small amount, but lots kept coming out from both ends. He was very dehydrated!

Mike was at his company stay-in meeting in a beach hotel of an internationally-renowned chain. He suspected the second meal there was the culprit that had caused his whole system to go mad. After going for more than a dozen times, I could see that he was showing signs of dehydration. With a strong dislike for hospitals and anything that comes with them (now, that is a whole different story), he was adamant in proving to me that he was actually having fun doing this new sport called toilet biathlon. The only one thing I could see sporty about this was that he was losing weight 'the natural way'. A few more times in and out of the toilet, Mike was ready to wave the white flag. Peak after-office hours on a Friday evening is not exactly a pleasant time to drive a very sick patient to hospital. My car was just short of a twirling red light and a siren as I drove past hundreds of cars, taking any left turns there were for short cuts.

Quite often we hear unbelievers say they are not ready to receive Jesus into their lives. One mid-aged man even added, "let me enjoy my life first and I'll consider Jesus when I'm old." One could only think the obvious as reason for this. God, gracious as He is, is no debtor as explained in Jesus' parable in the first half of Matthew 20. Whether we receive Christ early in life or on our death bed, God still accepts us and receives us into His Kingdom. He also does not care about the world's standard or rank of the person. Jesus showed that superiority is of no use when He embraced the little children into His Kingdom but rebuked the religious leaders and ruler.

Verses 6 and 7—"And about the eleventh hour he (the land owner) went out and found others standing idle, and said to them, 'Why have you been standing here idle all day?' They said to him, 'Because no one hired us.' He said to them, 'You also go into the vineyard, and whatever is right you will receive.'" Some only got to come into the Kingdom at the eleventh hour, as they had not heard the Gospel before that. Some were called at the third or sixth or ninth hour, but have rejected that call until the eleventh hour. He still received them all.

Then there are those who arrive earlier from the world (marketplace) into His Kingdom (vineyard), through time, become pompous or idle. An idle state is not something what God enjoys watching in anyone's life. Paul urged the Thessalonians to admonish the idle (1 Thessalonians 5:14). More warnings about idleness can be found in Proverbs 19:15 and 1 Timothy 5:13. Jesus emphasized this in the parable in verses 3 and 6 where it was as if the landowner was looking out specifically for people who were idle. Just like how God is calling *come, come, come out of the world. Life in My Kingdom is not a trifling decision and experience.*

Although it tells us here that there is a denarius set before us regardless of whether we start work in the vineyard at the third or the eleventh hour, we should also always be conscious to the fact that 'now' is always the time. When we do that, we will realise God's promise that life in His Kingdom is not a trifling experience is true. On the eleventh hour, we will then realize that we would not exchange the ten hours for anything. I know I would not.

When my car arrived at the accident&emergency entrance, Mike was taken into the emergency room immediately on a wheelchair. About fifteen minutes after the drip was administered, he knew he could have had it much better had he agreed to come in earlier.

*Tarrying has its consequences.*

# 27

# There's Room In The Inn

"And she brought forth her firstborn Son, and wrapped Him in swaddling cloths, and laid Him in a manger, because there was no room for them in the inn."

—Luke 2:7.

Since my younger days, I have been listening to Christmas sermons telling how Christians should not be caught up in the world's representation of Christmas. The fat guy in red, the prize for the tallest Christmas tree, the drinking and merry making, shopping, traditions . . . . the intrusive din of the world that is capable of robbing away the real holy meaning of the birth of Christ . . . . if we are not careful.

Believers think and plan of a more significant style of spending the season's days. So we see Christian groups preparing hard for a time of celebration, reaching out to friends with the message of Christmas. Then it is Church on Christmas morning with carols and a message of God's love coming to us in the form of Man. Well, my family and I have not done much differently from these in our way of celebrating Christmas the past many years.

This year, we had a strong prompting to agree to a 'Christmas with a difference' . . . .

I quote author and missionary Susan Warren to my family one of the days before Christmas: "I'm grateful to God who gave me a rich life, an incredible family, and the gift of salvation. I'm so grateful that He reached out of Heaven to the downtrodden, the lost, and the hungry people who didn't know Him, to give us eternal nourishment so we will hunger no more. This, I believe, is the true meaning of hospitality. I pray this Christmas season, you see the hospitality of Jesus Christ in your life." These words worked like a miracle in our hearts, that there was an immediate joyful response in unison and a firm like-mindedness to do what we actually did on Christmas Day.

December 25: We woke up to an early Christmas breakfast with three staying guests, who were experiencing this sort of Christmas morning for the first time. Christmas wishes were exchanged with joy. I prepared two plates of chocolate spice cake I baked the evening before, decorated the top with lemon cream and some Christmas cake decorations we see in the shops, and gave them to two of our neighbors. We wanted them to know that we gave and wished them Christ not because they have been good neighbors but because of Jesus. They were pleasantly surprised. We chatted and they started asking about our Christian faith.

About an hour later, the eight of us were on our way to visit some people, two of whom were celebrating their first Christmas as believers. The over-an-hour journey was filled with music and happy chats. Our hosts greeted us with gladness. We stayed with them for more than three hours. As we were coming home from our day's worth of Christmas difference, my daughter could not wait to post on her Facebook wall 'the best Christmas present is to bless people and see them smile because of it. This year was the most awesome Christmas'. When people are caught up in the excitement of their inner needs being met, I doubt they will remember anything else they have not received. Many a time, we misinterpret needs.

That's right, this Christmas our family did not attend Church but we brought the church to more than ten people. We did not go for a special Christmas lunch but we had meals that tasted exceptionally wonderful. We did not don our Christmas best but we clothed others with His love. We did not bring a bagful of presents to Church to give to friends but we gave the Gift which we have received.

More than 2000 years ago, there was no room for Jesus and His earthly parents at the inn. It need not have to remain that way today. I believe that what we are to the next person out there will tell if Jesus is special enough to always have room reserved for Him. For what we do, we do not unto ourselves, but unto Him. We all have different ways to remember and celebrate Christmas, but we should not forget who the focus of the celebration is.

*This Christmas, I have one song from the Gaithers'*
*Homecoming Christmas that has been stuck in my head:*
*Into the barn, into the world*
*Into the hearts of the boys and girls,*
*Never had a baby quite like Him,*
*Look who just checked in.*

*Has he checked in into your heart?*

# 28

# Ahh .... My Pillow, My Bed

After being very spoilt during my stay at the Sheraton Kowloon by every staff I came into contact with, the other two hotels after that were rated as just run-of-the-mill—my rating. Well, you can't blame me. Hotels like the Sheraton, Hilton, Pullman, Marriott, Ritz, and the like give a separate staff training on how to make their guests feel like they are worth a million. Maybe they don't do this training bit but it sure looks like it. These hotels are just short of putting a pea under layers of sheet to check if your stay is one which will make you come back again.

The Mandarin Singapore chain of hotels were part of my accommodation options when I travelled many years ago, being staff in one of their affiliations. During one of my travels, I arrived at the front desk of the Marina Mandarin to be told that they were running a 100% occupancy and my room had to be given up. Thoughts of annoyance were running through my head—yes, I was staff, and yes, customers should come first in this situation, but . . . . the front office manager interrupted my short moment of botheration, "However, Miss Tan", handing me the key, "We have prepared the presidential suite for you". Whoa! Not bad at all, I smiled professionally, doing a good job hiding my excitement. All that applesauce jazz about having given up my room was immediately forgiven.

Contrary to the many times of having indolently sprawled queen-like on thirty-inch (well, felt like it) thick super king size mattresses with prompt butler service at the sound of chime-like peals, I have also tasted the life of a typical Christian missionary in the interiors. One-room huts where everything was done in that one room—sleep, Bible study, cook, eat, fellowship, whatever else—and everything that went on outside the hut, I was encouraged and gave thanks for. I saw the important use of stilts, like those which supported our hut many feet up in the air, or wild boars would have been my house mates! I did not take baths in roman-designed sunken bath tubs en suite but I walked half a mile to dip myself in a river so murky I wondered if someone was competing with God who turned the water in the river into blood (Exodus 7:20), and changed the water into milk tea! I hunted for my meals among shrubs and shoots. A piece of chicken the size of 1/3 of my palm was a big treat during celebrations. A kerosene lamp was my light when darkness fell.

Luke 9:58—"And Jesus said to Him, 'foxes have holes and birds of the air have nests, but the Son of Man has nowhere to lay His head'" has many a time been used as a backup in sermons on leading a simple life as a Christian. This misinterpretation is easily believed because it is pointed to the account that Christ had lived on earth in poverty as He had said so in this verse. It was during one of Jesus' journeys on the road, that someone said to Him, 'Lord, I will follow You wherever You go' (verse 57), that Jesus was making sure that that someone knew what he was talking about when he said he would follow Jesus; the cost of discipleship. Not to be hasty and rash, and we mean to follow Christ, we need to count its cost. Whichever path Jesus may take us on, we need to lay aside the wants of the world. We shall not enter into this journey with Jesus to find ourselves seeking after earthly and temporal gains. There will also be persecution to look into. Because of partiality in beliefs, Christians may also be rejected, like Christ being refused hospitality in some towns He went into, which literally conveys an implication of having nowhere to lay His head.

It is not a Sheraton bed that gives me good sleep. Neither is it the two-inch mattress in a dilapidated hut in the interiors that makes me a great follower of Christ. It is when each time I lay my head on my pillow on the bed at the end of the day that reminds me to ask myself, "Have I counted the cost?"

*What is the cost of discipleship to you? May who Jesus is be worth so much more.*

# 29

# Water

If you are a mom and have not already spent more than half of your mom years telling your children to drink water, drink water, drink water, either you have already set up a device which repeats the command each time it detects a drop in body hydration or your children possess great knowledge in the cruciality of dehydration and they are not too busy to glug down 300ml of water every 1.5 hours without mom's telling them to do so. I do not have the device. My children know they need much water or they can fall sick, but they are too busy trying to conquer Venus to stop for a drink of water.

We can still live after a week without food, but we could die in a few days without water. Hence, the catchphrase 'I'm dying of thirst', I guess. According to reports, the human brain is made up of 95% water, blood is 82% and lungs 90%. A mere 2% drop in our body's water supply can trigger signs of dehydration, like fatigue, difficulty in focusing, fuzzy memory and some other health issues. Water aids in digestion and most of all the other body processes. It lubricates our joints and helps control body temperature. The list goes on about why water is so needed for a healthy body.

Water is needed for other physical uses too. It helps us clean, gives us exercise, beautifies, transports, etc. When God decided that the surface of the earth He created would be about 70% covered with water, you would think He had a special liking for water. Is that also why the word *water* or its equivalent is used much in His holy Word?

In the Bible, we read of many amazing happenings which have taken place that involved water. God parted the waters to save the Israelites from the hands of the Egyptians (Exodus 14:21-31). A Syrian army commander called Naaman dipped himself seven times in the Jordan (water) and he was healed from leprosy (2 Kings 5:14). Jesus was baptized in the Jordan which marked the beginning of His ministry (Matthew 3:13-17). John 4 reports the meeting at Jacob's well between Jesus and the Samaritan woman, from whom our Lord asked for a drink. After a soul-searching dialogue, Jesus offered Himself as the Living Water, which changed the woman's life, and then many of the Samaritans in the city believed in Jesus through the woman's testimony.

Two *water* verses have chiefly unbolted the depths of me in the book of John. Chapter 4 verse 14 states "But whoever drinks of the water that I shall give him will never thirst. But the water that I shall give him will become in him a fountain of water springing up into everlasting life". This water is not literally the transparent tasteless liquid that comes out of our pipes, for whatever waters we drink, we shall thirst again. But Jesus is showing here that whoever partakes of the love and grace that the Spirit of God offers us, along with His promises in the Gospel, shall never be in want. So gentle, yet so powerful. I see a *water* that is beautiful like a fountain springing up is very powerful to destroy sin.

When we believe, the goodness of God's *water* will flow into our lives. Its cleansing and purifying process begins its work on our human habits, attitudes, behaviors, likes and dislikes; the process having to do with the blood of Jesus cleansing our whole being from all sin. This *water* refreshes those who have been burnt with life's harsh realities. The downcast are being revived, springing back to life, walking uprightly on the path of eternal life. As we believe and receive, unending large measures of His love and grace will keep filling our lives causing them to flow out again. This outflowing will be evident in our lives' nature to disseminate. "He who believes in Me, as the Scripture has said, out of his heart will flow rivers of living water" (John 7:38).

I'm getting myself a drink. Water, anyone?

*How is your body's hydration? How is your spirit's hydration?*

# 30

# In Other Words

$B$*illions of blue blistering barnacles!* Now, if you have been a fan of classic Belgian comic books by Herge, you will be familiar with Captain Archibald Haddock's sui generis turn of phrases, and that I am not cursing someone for stepping onto my cucumber patch. Without Captain Haddock, Tintin's adventures would be less high-spirited; more calm maybe but if you are one like I am, who is into Tintin once in a while, coiling into my cave for a slightly childlike flavor in life, you will agree that Tintin's adventures need someone like Captain Haddock. After all, it is an adventure! He is usually in his angry and agitated disposition, perhaps brought about by his love for whiskey, which eventually makes him a creative man in cuss words. It may be entertaining to the readers but I have found myself sometimes in that imprecating tone when something happens in the spur of the moment and occurring plans foiled.

When we are not careful with things we hear or read, and allow the words to own a place in our conscious mind, they may give birth to a nature that is not nurturing to our inner man. This, in turn, will be like a tiny rock caught in our shoe in our relationship with God. It does not stop with us. We stain the lives around us and we confuse others who have yet to know God.

My children were using some words and phrases which made me feel uneasy, coupled with certain behavior patterns which disturbed me too. My first reaction was "since when did you start . . . ." and "where did you learn to . . . .". Their reply was obvious that they never realized these were happening. I later found out that youth leaders they were mixing around with displayed the same characteristics. Being children, they will tend to follow what other older folks say and do, most of the time unawares. It is even of more importance when those they follow are people they look up to as leaders. Their parents are not exempted from this crucial role.

I was perturbed. Do my children have to be around leaders like these for the rest of their youth years? Do I just sit back and watch my children go deeper into such nonsense? There are many things around us wherever we go which we cannot avoid. But what we can do to avoid those things, we do. God wants us to be heedful to His words of wisdom, so let us see what His Word says about this:

"Death and life are in the power of the tongue, and those who love it will eat its fruit."—Proverbs 18:21.

"But those things which proceed out of the mouth come from the heart, and they defile a man."—Matthew 15:18.

"Let no corrupt word proceed out of your mouth, but what is good for necessary edification, that it may impart grace to the hearers."—Ephesians 4:29.

"If anyone among you thinks he is religious, and does not bridle his tongue but deceives his own heart, this one's religion is useless."—James 1:26.

. . . . and the list goes on. James 1:26 tells of the vanity of our belief when we take pains in ceremonial and other ways telling others we are believers, but not bridling our tongue.

*Oh, I must read this chapter to myself too.*

# 31

# To Meet Or Not To Meet

As we gather may Your Spirit work within us,
As we gather may we glorify Your name;
Knowing well that as our hearts begin to worship,
We'll be blessed because we came.

—Maranatha Music.

Last week I was contemplating on whether to go for a women's fellowship. After days of sprinting and bolting from one destination to another, coupled with extra chores, I just wanted to have some *me* time. Just the night before the meeting, I decided I should go. After all, this could be a *me* time . . . . with other women who were also looking for their own *me* time. So I went for the women's fellowship and I am glad I did. We had encouraging moments of sharing, a serious time in worshiping God with songs, a filling study on the book of Ruth, a good dose of prayer, and afterward fellowship round the dining table. I met some old friends and made a few new ones. I was blessed because I went.

Shouldn't it be like this when we go for a time of fellowship, a church service, a Bible study, or any type of meeting that involves God's people and ministries, and the Holy Spirit? I will say yes, it should. It must. When such gatherings are filled and inspired by God, there is no space for a spirit that feels the opposite, wondering what he or she is doing there. It is like when a liquid is flowing intravenously in our veins. We will know that His Spirit is at work in that meeting.

On the contrary, there are also ministry or leaders meetings where more often than not, and sad to say, attendees are at each other's throats. No one expects everybody to be of the same way of thinking or of the same opinion, but do we have to behave unfittingly in God's ministries? When we give God our word that we will serve in the position or ministry, our word is not enough; our whole being comes along with it. That includes our attitude and behaviour. I have also been to Bible study meetings where eating takes up more of the entire effort than anything else. Ate before meeting, ate during meeting, and ate some more after meeting! Then distasteful idle talks were sprinkled here and there like seasonings over food, with no forethought of the presence of a visitor or a new believer. Agendas like these impair the appearance of what a Christian meeting ought to be.

If our meetings are not representing our God, what are they representing? If our worship service does not place significance in our worship for God; if our leaders meeting consists more of other goings-on than what a Christian leaders meeting should actually have for the good of the management of God's church; if our prayer meeting appears like they need to be called chatting or eating meeting instead then we really need to have a reality check. Do our meetings involve the Holy Spirit, or are we only going through the motion of having meetings? Are we guilty of pushing His help away? When we plan for a meeting, is it our agenda or God's? Stuffing churchy word or Bible-sounding program here and there make up a scant regard for its spiritual purpose.

The Holy Spirit proceeds from the Father: "When the Helper comes, whom I shall send to you from the Father, the Spirit of truth who proceeds from the Father, He will testify of Me."—John 15:26.

The Holy Spirit proceeds from Christ: "Nevertheless, I tell you the truth. It is to your advantage that I go away; for if I do not go away, the Helper will not come to you; but if I depart, I will send Him to You."—John 16:7.

May our meetings be *not* going through an ichabod experience, but those which testify of Jesus!

*What happened at your last meeting?*

# 32

# From God's Perfumery

My husband and children were complaining about the smell, with my daughter commenting that soon our guests would think that our house was perpetually with someone doing one thing or another in the bathroom. I lost one vote to four, so out went the bokashi compost buckets to the backyard. To me, it was just a whiff here and there of the unwanted raw foods which i used for making natural fertilizer for the plants.

I, too, find certain smells repulsive. Cigarette smoke, pungent bad body odor and vehicle exhaust fumes are some of the smells that make me peevish. At a breath of any of these, all sensitivities within me automatically put my brain and lungs in a state of alert. The opposite is also true when my nose detects pleasant scents from flowers or essential oils, or an aroma of fresh bakes when I step into a charming cottage style patisserie. Oh, these perk up the depths of me.

Scents have a peculiar characteristic. They stay and linger on, some for a long time. They jolt memories. They encourage. They can be so spirituous that you want to follow the trail they make. Our lives as God's children should also give out a kind of scent. A genuine and reliable Christianity lived is always pouring out a fragrance that is pleasing to God. Our Father in Heaven loves to inhale such pleasant scents of His children because this type of fragrance can only result from one thing—knowing Christ personally, and testifying to it, and living it out.

2 Corinthians 2:14-15—"Now thanks be to God who always leads us in triumph in Christ, and through us diffuses the fragrance of His knowledge in every place. For we are to God the fragrance of Christ . . . ." Please tell me if you are not spiritually adrenalized that God has already rescued you from the clutches of a contaminated world; that He is willing to be evident in your life for the world to see. Ezekiel 20:41—"I will accept you as a sweet aroma when I bring you out from the peoples and gather you out of the countries where you have been scattered; and I will be hallowed in you before the Gentiles." But this will not be true if we were to, after being cleansed by the blood of Jesus Christ, go back to the world, as written in Proverbs 26:11—"As a dog returns to his own

vomit, so a fool repeats his folly." In the eyes of the other person, our lives can be emitting a sweet fragrance or a bad odor.

Whenever I leave a wet market, I notice a lingering fishy smell on my clothes, skin and hair. That makes up practically the whole physical me. My body picks up the smell and hangs on to it until I wash it off. It can be like this when we let ourselves hang around for long surroundings that smell opposing to the sweet fragrance of Christ. It is like pigs wallowing in the mud. There is not a spot on the pig that is not covered with dirt. If we are careless or lazy, that filth will start sticking all over us.

Let us be God's children who are always walking around emitting the sweet fragrance of His love, His peace, His joy; a powerful scent that leaves a trail that others want to follow.

*If you are a fragrance produced from God's perfumery, keep your bottle capped securely. Do not lose that scent.*

Herb scones
Cheese spread
Chinese wolf berries
Peach Tea

# 33

# Breathe And Remember Life

Lina was on her way home in the evening after work. Just like any other day, she was driving along the coastal highway. And just like any other day, she was listening to her favorite radio station and thinking of her family who are waiting for her to have dinner together. Just like any other day, her car drove by the construction site of the second Penang bridge ramp. But unlike any other day when she would just drive pass the scaffolding where the road narrowed to a single lane, she did not make it pass that part last Thursday. As her car was going under those steel bars weighing thousands of ton, something gave way and we could only wish that it was just a filming of a stunt in an action movie! Within seconds, Lina's car was crushed under the heap of heavy steel.

My family and I were at a birthday dinner when we heard the news of the fallen scaffolding. That was the site we passed on our way to our friend's. I recalled looking at the car clock when we passed that area. I don't know if there was a Lina among those killed in the nasty accident, and if there was someone in the family waiting for her for dinner. I could only allow that imaginative part of me to think that something like that was happening with one of those who died. He or she did not know that the next second would be the last breath. When I heard the news, I felt numb for a while.

The psalmist described the delicateness of man's life: "As for man, his days are like grass; as a flower of the field, so he flourishes. For the wind passes over it, and it is gone, and its place remembers it no more" (Psalm 103:15-16). We see how unpredictable man's life is. It is endowed with tremendous gifts and beauty, yet it is, like the grass and flowers of the field, so vulnerable to the dangers of its surrounding. James 4:14 gives a self-explanatory reminder: "Whereas you do not know what will happen tomorrow. For what is your life? It is even a vapor that appears for a little time and then vanishes away." If we are conscious that life on earth is uncertain, and such precious and costly breath we take every few seconds, we will do what we ought to do here on earth and we will not do some things we have been doing . . . .

Hurt, bitterness, anger and grudge are worthless to hold on to. Jealousy, evil scheming, and unforgiveness take up way too much space in this precious life, bearing bad fruits. All these, and still many more rob away life's beauty, causing damage to the max. If we think about life in the right way, we put away self-absorbedness and greediness, and in their place, we want to be giving. We pursue a life that touches other lives. We desire to live a life that is evidence of Christlikeness. We will want to use our time, and hence lead our children to do the same, to spell l-i-f-e.

There was a man God had allowed to see and taste life from most perspectives. He thought of many experiences he had lived through on earth and came up with a conclusion that "All is vanity" (Ecclesiastes 1:2, and throughout the book). If we were to ask this wisest man who ever lived, Solomon, he would reply, "Let us hear of the conclusion of the whole matter: Fear God and keep His commandments, for *this is man's all*. For God will bring every work into judgment, including every secret thing, whether good or evil" (Ecclesiastes 12:13-14). When we do this, we are not living life in vain.

The news reported that the accident occurred around 7pm. Our car passed that area when our car clock showed 6.58pm.

*"Thank you, God, for physical life here on earth. Help us to make it what You intend it to be. Thank You for eternal spiritual life through Jesus."*

# 34

# Never Too Old

"Let everything that has breath praise the LORD. Praise the LORD!"

—Psalm 150:6.

All this while my friend from India had thought that I was many years younger than my real age. It would be unappreciative to correct her so I smiled and basked in that esteem for a while. As pathetic as it may sound, at my age, the brain automatically shifts a remark like this one to become a compliment in having age-defying looks. My friend said she would not have guessed that I was just a short distance away from fifty if I had not told her so. To her, I am too active to be at this age. In her hometown, those who have crossed over forty consider themselves to be old. These passive midlifers, weary of life, have lost much vigor in most of life's passion. It pulls a person down to a mere simple routine day after day.

I was (and still am) truly encouraged by an elderly couple I remember as Uncle and Aunty Choo who were still serving in Church in their old age. I recall seeing them, during my youth days, moving slowly but courageously around Church doing the things they could help in. They never failed to greet those they passed by with a warm smile. I never heard them complain. Their enthusiasm in life made me think that they would live forever on earth. Such zeal in Christian lives reflects what Paul told the Romans when he preached about how Christians should lead transformed lives. We should not go alongside the world in its slothfulness in living this precious gift from God, but we ought to be "not lagging in diligence, fervent in spirit, serving the Lord;" (Romans 12:11), among other key attributes of our changed lives.

When we enter into God's Kingdom, He ignites in us a love so powerful we never would have known existed. All the testimonies and Christian cliches we have heard before become factual. In Psalm 104:33-34, the psalmist committed to sing to God as long as he lived, and while he had his being. When we live in God's perfect love that is eternal, this means there is no ending to our being alive in our physical and spiritual self while here on earth, and later on in Heaven too. We do this not with our own strength but in His strength because He is the one sustaining us and He is the one championing our course. There is no stopping us when we live in this assurance. We may be advance in our earthly age, but we do not stop singing of the life which is given by God. We may go through some tough times along the way but we still have that living in us to be glad in Him.

Do you have breath? . . . . Then praise the Lord!

Last Sunday, a 10-year-old in Children's Church called me *jie jie* (big sister in Chinese, as a way of respect to a female who is your generation but older). Agewise, that is stretching things quite a bit . . . . well, I don't mind stretching . . . .

*The joy of the Lord is my strength.*

# 35

# The Joy Of Having Found And Being Found

I can imagine the excitement and joy in the woman who eventually found her lost coin. This was evident in her calling out to her friends and neighbors to come rejoice with her on her find. This is a parable which Jesus told as an illustration to what it is like in the presence of the angels of God over each sinner who repents. In Luke 15, our creative Lord related more parable in *the lost sheep* and *the lost son* to show immense significance of our soul being so loved by Him.

On the other side, can you remember the time when you found that particular thing you had been looking for? That special kind of someone? Or that feeling of suitability for a specific career or Christian ministry? Or simply that certain way a cafe made your favorite food? Would you wish to relive that feeling of excitement that comes with a purpose? Well, I would.

I have been searching and searching for my lost music. My *Jose Mari Chan* and *Danny Chan Pak Keung* cassette tapes are missing from my small collection. These were part of my teenage and young adulthood music collection. My friend, who also enjoyed *Danny Chan Pak Keung's* songs, and I used to listen to a few of his songs during our younger 'let it all hang out' moments. I have searched in my home and have also gone back to my parents' to look for them but it has been in vain. I have planned to upgrade these two music albums to CD status like I have done with my other old music like ABBA, Air Supply, Bee Gees, to name a few.

I am thankful that I have searched and found Truth. God is now my refuge. Indeed in countless times He has proven to be my strength and my song. With His boundless love He has paved the way for me to walk on. I have found that by just being called a Christian is not enough. We need to experience God through our relationship with Him. We can read the Bible that there is God, but that is not relationship. We can learn about the history of biblical times and memorize the events that come chronologically but it still does not bring us into that special love partnership with God. He wants us to be aware of Him in all circumstance. I know of people who can mock God and His Word outrightly, agreeing with anti-God views, and even spend good money on books that ridicule the Almighty God. Then when something unpleasant happens in their lives, they start clicking on 'like' on motivational posts in Facebook that have the word *God* in them. I say these are people who are stung by their own mockery!

By the way, if you know where I can get the albums I mentioned, I would appreciate a note form you. Meanwhile, I guess I will just have to remind myself about the parable of the lost coin as my hope that one day I will find my lost music.

*Have you found God? "I say to you that likewise there will be more joy in Heaven over one sinner who repents than over ninety-nine just persons who need no repentance."— Luke 15:7.*

# 36

# An Invitation Not To Be Ignored.

Many months ago, we invited some friends over for a home-cooked Indian dinner. One of our friends said he would take a rain check because he had to entertain some visiting guests. Last week, we invited a few friends for a home-cooked Nyonya (an Asian mixed parentage) dinner. Again, the same friend could not make it as he already had a prior engagement. Our friend then suggested that I got busy with my wok and ladle again soon for another home-cooked dinner get-together. Hmm, I'll see about that. Maybe next time, he will have to grease my palm by agreeing to wash up a greasy kitchen after dinner.

In a parable (Luke 14: 16-24), Jesus told about a certain man giving a great supper and invited many. These guests had already been told of the invite long before the day of the banquet. When everything was ready for his guests' enjoyment, one by one his guests started making excuses for not being able to go. Although each man's preoccupation was different from the next person's, all were found shamming to put off their presence at the banquet. Putting myself in host position, I would be angered by such irresponsibleness coupled with cheap shot excuses.

The doubts and reluctance of those who brushed off Gospel offers carry a taste of contempt toward the God of Heaven, and this rightly angers Him. How many times the Jewish nation saw the miracles and other forms of proof to know for sure that Jesus was the long-awaited Messiah, but they chose to forsake the approach of Christ's patient and loving grace. When this happened, the apostles were told to switch their focus to the Gentiles, and with these Gentiles the church was filled (verses 21-24). All that God has prepared for our benefits in the Gospel was not meant for a fruitless outcome. He had a purpose and that purpose was going to work. His church would be filled. If what is offered to us is neglected, others will accept with gratefulness.

You may decline a friend's invite today; it is alright, it will only cost you a meal. Moreover, you may even be invited back on another day. Rejecting God's invite for a ministry, anything God is blessing you with, salvation in the Lord Jesus, or any kind of opportunity to bring glory to His name, you could be missing it all. It could even cost you a whole future.

It is God's house. We do not knock on His door anytime we want and demand it to be opened at our convenience. "When once the Master of the House has risen up and shut the door, and you begin to stand outside and knock at the door, saying, 'Lord, Lord, open for us', and He will answer and say to you, 'I do not know you, where you are from', then you will begin to say, 'we ate and drank in Your presence, and You taught in our streets.' But He will say, 'I tell you, I do not know you, where you are from. Depart from Me, all you workers of iniquity.'"—Luke 13:25-27.

Just think, how many people will be self-assured that they should be saved only to be rejected on the day of trial, for their self-confidence has deceived them so.

*Look at an invitation from both sides. Imagine you as the host. Imagine you as the guest.*

# 37

# What's Your Position?

My eldest child, Rebekah said she was at her wits' end with the nonchalant attitudes of her two younger siblings where responsibilities were concerned. When she chided them for their insouciant ways to their chores, their response was not befitting one talking to an older person. Since that was not the first time they had behaved in such a way toward her advising them, she cried to me about how she was not being respected as their big sister. While I comforted her and asked her to be more patient with the younger ones, I scolded Hannah and Joshua for being disrespectful.

I emphatize with Rebekah because I understand her position, for I am also the big sister. Although I did not have it as hard while I was growing up as she does now, I know how she feels when she is being treated unfairly where her birthright as their big sister is concerned. Knowing our position in our family is significant. I have also reminded my son not to take advantage of his position as the youngest child and only son to get his way, which is the norm in most Asian families, and that I would not tolerate a spoilt brat attitude.

From another perspective, to be assured of one's position is an added confidence in life. I grew up with a father who instilled many positive stories of our Chinese family name clan in olden days China that I only wanted to marry another Tan when I grew up. Although I eventually got over the straightforward childlike belief, I was still strongly convinced then that Tan was one of the elite clans if I were to go back to search my roots in China. Whenever I did something well, or someone complimented me on something, my father would add that I was a Tan. I felt my name initials had to remain that way for the rest of my life, or it would spoil everything which I had my initials 'RT' or 'GT' on. Such was that much confidence of my position in life I got parental influence on.

I prayed to ask Jesus to come into my life when I was 14. I was enjoying life as a new Christian then but I never realized the great significance of holding that position as God's child until years later into my adulthood. David's Psalm in 139:13,14 suddenly appeared so remarkably clear to me that "For You formed my inward parts; You covered me in my mother's womb. I will praise You, for I am fearfully and wonderfully made; . . . .". Wow, God, I thought, I feel so perfect in Your hands. I might not have perfectly straight teeth, I might not have been the best Physics student in school, I might not have been accepted by that institution, but You make me feel beautiful—beautiful in Your sight. That is what God took so much care in making me. Now, that is a position anyone will want to have in life!

Another verse that tells God's caring hands upon our lives is Jeremiah 29:11—"'For I know the thoughts that I think toward you', says the LORD, 'thoughts of peace and not of evil, to give you a future and a hope'". When we are at a position where we feel hopeless, down in the dumps, wondering why situations have turned out the way they did, this is a promise to hold on to. I have been there, and knowing that God allowed that to happen in order for His good wonderful will to happen in my life for my good, the burden was nothing that I would want to hold on to.

Other awesome promises form God to grasp: Isaiah 40:29-31, Philippians 4:19, Romans 8:37-39, John 14:27, Proverbs 1:33, and many more. When we know God and are assured of our position in Him, we can be rested in many situations in life. We will not be worried that people are talking about us. We will not be holding on to what is obviously not God's will like a security blanket. We will not be or do all these simply because we know of our undeniable position in God. There is no place for insecurity and uncertainty because God is our all-powerful security.

*What is your position?*

✦ *If life has pulled you down, I hope that this will help you to realise that you are actually worth far more than what you are feeling about yourself now.*

✦ *If you know deep inside you have been living a life that is self-glorifying, it is my prayer that this has been a humbling read.*

# 38

# All-In-One

If you are in deep waters, circumstances are caving in,
Maybe you feel neglected, rejected and deserted;
I'll tell you about a Man, in this state many have put Him in,
But you need not stay like this because for you He had shed his blood.

If your marriage is not looking too promising,
You are opting for an unfavorable conclusion, hold on!;
I'll tell you about a Groom, His bride He adores,
Make Him the focus in your union, no more forlorn.

If your children's ways are driving you up the wall,
Parenting seems way too much to bear;
I'll tell you about a Father who loves with grace,
Follow Him, and you'll see home with warmth and care.

If your work is ruthlessly overloading,
You're burdened and lots are piling up mercilessly;
I'll tell you about a Helper whose help none can do without,
Ask Him; your load He'll lighten and more joyful you'll be.

You may think there are just too many to get to know,
the Man, the Groom, the Father, the Helper; O, grunt!;
You see, they are but only One, I'm not kidding,
That's what you get when you believe in my God, all in One!

You've been missing out big time, I'm telling ya,
If you don't already know this wonderful God;
Offer food, shave head, pierce body, you need not do,
These are futile when by His blood you've been bought.

O, you've known Him for years, you say?,
But why is He still only a God in the book of old?;
This God I'm talking about is of mind, spirit and soul,
Seek Him relationally, many things to you He'll unfold.

*Do you know Him?*

# 39

# Do You Prune Or Ax?

"And Jesus came and spoke to them, saying, 'All authority has been given to Me in Heaven and on earth. Go therefore, and make disciples of all the nations, baptizing them in the name of the Father, and of the Son and of the Holy Spirit, teaching them to observe all things that I have commanded you; and lo, I am with you always, even to the end of the age.' Amen."—Matthew 28:18-20.

Four months ago a few of my Japanese okra seedlings looked like they needed to be in the ICU. They were wilting away. I did not give up hope despite the hot weather which I guess was the main cause of the shriveling stems and leaves. I set up umbrellas when the sun was scorching hot and when the rain was too much for them to bear. Slowly, after weeks of TLC, I started to see new shoots and the stems were straightening up and fattening. While doing all these, the growth of the seedlings was part of my prayer to God. I also prayed over them while watering my baby plants. Today, flowers and fresh pods are a normal sight all over my okra patch. I reap good fruits every 2-3 days.

I liken this to the process of discipling someone. I recall an incident which turned out to be a disheartening experience in a lady's search for help and Truth. When I started to disciple her in her new life in Christ, she related her story . . . .

Jane (not her real name) was already at the end of the rope in a very complicating situation at home when one day she decided to drive out to nowhere. She told herself to keep driving, and maybe she could turn up at a place where there would be help for a breakthrough.

After a long drive, she saw a church in front of her. There was a slight jolt of excitement that maybe she would be able to get someone in that building to listen to her and help her. She was captivated by the sereneness of the place as she drove into the compound of the church. The heritage look of the building gave her a sense of calm. It seemed old enough to contain all the help an emotionally torn person lacked. Jane parked her car and boldly stepped into the office and asked to see someone whom she could talk to. The person she tried to relate the predicament she was facing to was not too interested to be involved in her 'mess'. The talk was very short; I guess enough to let the doctor start diagnosing and prescribing. Well, it looked that way! The person took out a book and told her to go home and read it. No sharing of the Gospel? No praying with Jane? No caring Christian advice? No asking her to come back soon to check on her progress? Jane left . . . . and went home to square one.

When I heard this, I was disturbed. Surely there could have been much more to offer than just a book. There are many verses in the Bible which tell us to reach out, make disciples, and, teach and disciple one another. One of the most significant passages is the Great Commission (Matthew 28:18-20) which Jesus gave to His disciples on the mountain. I believe this assignment, this charge, was not only for the apostles to undertake at that time, but also for all Christians today who would follow Him. From what I have been personally observing, many Christians take these verses for granted, even preachers. It has become so familiar and obvious in the mission context that it no longer captures that congregation's passion. Most Christians instantly think of one word when these verses are uttered: mission. Their minds take them to places of nowhere near, and they hold meetings to plan for the programs, gifts and other logistics for the mission trip to be successful . . . . but when God put the mission field right under their noses, all they do is toss a book over.

So what do we do with people who are genuinely in need of help; Christians and unbelievers alike? Do we throw them a book? Or do we go to them with a heart of Jesus?

Quoting Ravi Zacharias, Christian author and speaker: "Though we continue to exist, we miss life for what it was meant to be."

*In God's garden, let's prune.*

# 40

# Exercise Daily . . . .
# Walk With The Lord

For two days last week I had the rare privilege of working out in the gym. Our daughter, Hannah was in a competition two months ago and her team emerged as state champ so they went on to the national level. This year the nationals was held in one of the southern states in our country. My husband and I, like what most proud parents of a creative and talented teenager would have done, drove 370 miles to give support. While there, time was moving wonderfully downtempo that I thought I would make believe for a while that I was on Fantasy Island. No chores, no appointments to rush to, no chauffeuring children . . . . why not! It was good to feel like a chicken with a head for five days. I went to the gym.

I was a gym enthusiast during my pre-marriage days. I was in circuit training. Oh, those gym days. The weights, the bars, bikes, free exercises . . . . they keep you going from the brain down to the tendons inside your feet.

That is our physical gym. What about our spiritual gym? The basic practical characteristics of a Christian's lifestyle—the daily habits like prayer and Bible reading, the fruit of the Spirit attitude, the dying to self, the understanding of living under God's grace and living it out . . . . they keep you going from the head down to the toes. If one has been a Christian long enough to know and experience the difference between active spiritual habit days and inactive ones, he will not choose to go back to days of spiritual indolence. I have heard complains over and over again about how hard it can be to get into good Christian habits and stay that way. Yours truly have fallen into such guilty trap before. In the concerns of tight schedules, many a time I had not spared myself in the area of being in His presence enough. When this sort of habit set into routine, I eventually realized a certain heaviness in my spirit. Just like how our toned muscles slowly loosen into flab when we stop using or exercising them, so felt I the slowness and pudginess in my spiritual life when I allow time for God's matters to be compromised.

When schedules around us get too overwhelmed, we may notice a downhill slide in daily Christian habits, which, when happens often enough, can accumulate into a downhill slide in our attitudes and behaviors too. Patience may soon be lacking, and anger takes its place. Logical Christian thinking may lose its hold to worldly views. This may slowly make us (inadvertently?) forget that we have the Spirit of God living in us and we may not care so much about working out our salvation with fear and trembling (Philippians 2:12-13) anymore, co-operating with God for His will to work in us. Be careful, because spiritual idleness causes us to lose our weapon to quench the seething darts of the evil one.

Spotted on a stationery: 'Exercise Daily—Walk With The Lord'. Couldn't have been more appropriately said.

"Therefore take up the whole armor of God, that you may be able to withstand in the evil day, and having done all, to stand. Stand therefore, having girded your waist with truth, having put on the breastplate of righteousness, and having shod your feet with the preparation of the Gospel of peace; above all, taking the shield of faith with which you will be able to quench all the fiery darts of the wicked one. And take the helmet of salvation, and the sword of the Spirit, which is the Word of God.—Ephesians 6:13-17.

You know, those two days of gym have kinda whetted my appetite for a gym comeback. And you can bet on it that I'm pretty excited about it.

*If, at this point in your life, everything to do with the Lord seems far away, I would like to challenge you to stand up again. Shake off the cobwebs and say to God that you are going to get rid of that ugly paunch of spiritual idleness. I want to encourage you that you need not have to do this alone. You have the benefit of counting on the grace of God. His abundant grace which is already in you will quicken your endeavor.*

I hope you have been blessed

with what I have shared

in this book.


Do you know

how much you are worth

in God's eyes?

Look at the Niagara Falls,

the Swiss Alps,

the Amazon Rainforest,

the Pacific Ocean,

the stars of the Constellation Orion;

YOU are worth an infinity more than those to Him.

Yes, even more than berries and scones

. . . . with a dollop of cream!

# Cream Scones

*3 cups flour*

*2 tablespoons baking powder*

*3 teaspoons sugar*

*3/4 teaspoon salt*

*6 tablespoons butter*

*3 large eggs*

*1/2 cup cream*

*Mix and sift dry ingredients.*

*Work on butter with fingertips into dry ingredients for a crumbly feel.*

*Add beaten eggs and cream to make dough pliable but firm to handle. Add more cream if needed.*

*Turn dough out onto floured board. Roll dough into 1 inch thick.*

*Cut into 16-20 pieces with a knife. Arrange cut pieces two inches apart on a lightly greased pan.*

*Sprinkle with icing sugar after giving the top of each piece a light brush of egg-white (optional).*

*Bake for 15-20 minutes at 430F/220C.*

# Old English Drop Scones

*3 cups flour*

*4 tablespoons caster sugar*

*1 1/2 cups milk*

*2 eggs*

*2 teaspoons bicarbonate soda*

*3 teaspoons cream of tartar*

*2 tablespoons soft butter*

* Beat sugar, half the milk and eggs together.
* Add sifted flour, bicarbonate soda
and cream of tartar. Mix well.
* Slowly add the remainder of milk. Fold in
the butter. Batter should be not runny.
* Scoop and drop batter two inches or
so apart on lightly greased pan.
* Bake for about 20 minutes at 390F/200C,
or until scones are light golden brown.

Makes 15 pieces.

Other ideas:

* Add a few drops of extract (vanilla, lemon,
orange, mint, or almond) to batter.
* Use a greased frying pan instead of the oven.

# About The Author:

Women's ministry, discipling, event management, and, family and parenting events are few of the phrases one can associate with Gina Tan. With a God-given passion in seeing women lead successful lives in the Lord and a special love for the people she disciples and counsels, Gina has led many to Christ. A helper wife to her husband in their family and a doting mother to her three children, she has God to thank for in her achievements in life.